A SCORCHING HOT TIME IN SUDAN

A Relief Worker's Stories from Inside an African Refugee Camp

By Richard Leutzinger

PublishAmerica
Baltimore

First printing

At the specific preference of the author, PublishAmerica allowed this work to remain exactly as the author intended, verbatim, without editorial input.

ISBN: 1-4241-0288-X
PUBLISHED BY PUBLISHAMERICA, LLLP
www.publishamerica.com
Baltimore

Printed in the United States of America

For Margaret

THE HORN OF AFRICA

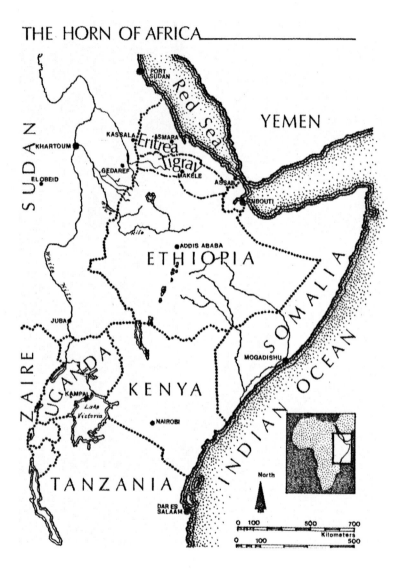

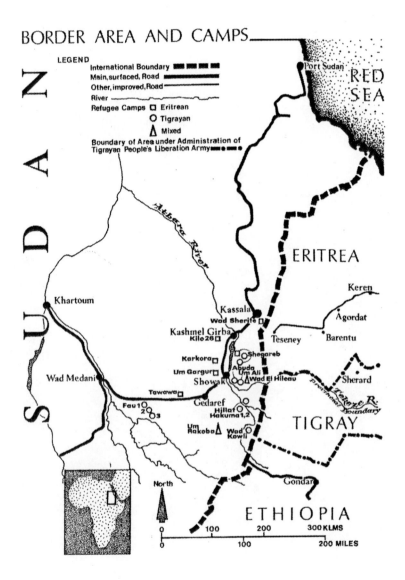

BORDER AREA AND CAMPS

LEGEND

International Boundary
Main, surfaced, Road
Other, improved, Road
River
Refugee Camps □ Eritrean
 ○ Tigrayan
 △ Mixed
Boundary of Area under Administration of
Tigrayan People's Liberation Army

SUDAN

Atbara River

Khartoum

Kassala
Wad Sherife □
Kashmel Girba ○
Kilo 26 □
Karkora □
Um Gargur □   Shegareb
Wad Medani   Abuda
Tawawa □   Um Ali
Fau 1 ○   △ Wad El Hileau
2 ○ 3 ○   Showak
Gedaref
Hillat
Hakuma 1,2
Um
Rakoba △   Wad
Kowli

RED SEA

Port Sudan

ERITREA

Keren

Agordat

Teseney   Barentu

Sherard

Setit R.
Provisional
Boundary

TIGRAY

Gondar

ETHIOPIA

North

0   100   200   300 KLMS
0   100   200 MILES

ONE

I knew it would be hot in Sudan. I knew some days would be unbearably hot. But I didn't count on it being quite this hot.

I arrived in Khartoum, the capital, sometime after midnight following a flight up the Nile and across the Nubian Desert from Cairo, where I had stopped for three days to see the pyramids and get acclimated to the weather. It took me only one day in Cairo to decide I had overreacted to weeks of warnings about the African heat. I enjoyed it there from the very beginning.

Temperatures were in the 90s and every few blocks, it seemed, there was a juice bar where for a few piasters you could quench your thirst on the freshly squeezed juice of oranges, grapefruit, strawberries, sugarcane or carrots. There were also vendors selling *kakadina*, a drink made from ice water and hibiscus flowers. And there were more tea shops than juice vendors, where for even fewer piasters, you could get a small glass of sweet hot tea with fresh mint leaves. There was no need to go thirsty while exploring Cairo on foot.

My Sudan Airways flight from Cairo to Khartoum was scheduled to leave at 9:00 o'clock at night. That seemed an odd departure time for a 3 ½-hour flight, but I'd been told there was less turbulence flying over the desert in the cool of night. Sudan Airways had a reputation as an odd airline anyway. It was often spoken of among travelers in half-Arabic, half-English as *Mumkin* (Maybe) Airways, *Bukkra* (Tomorrow) Air, *Insha'allah* (God Willing) Airways, and *Malesh* Airlines. *Malesh* is a favorite Sudanese expression meaning: who cares...never mind...it doesn't matter...so what?...what can you do?

We took off at 8:30 p.m., not 9:00 o'clock. However, we didn't leave 30 minutes early, we left 23 ½ hours late. All information about the delay was veiled in secrecy until two hours before takeoff. Until then, there was no Sudan Airways plane on the ground at the airport in Cairo, no one there knew where the plane was, and no one knew when it would turn up or when it would depart again.

Bob Medrala, the American Refugee Committee's representative who eventually met me at the airport in Khartoum, hadn't been able to get any information about my flight at his end either until 10 minutes before I landed. No one had been authorized to tell him (or maybe no one in the air terminal there knew) the plane would be a whole day late. The reason, it turned out: there wasn't enough gas to fly the plane from Khartoum to Cairo so it could fly us back from Cairo to Khartoum.

I was relieved to find Bob waiting at the airport when I finally arrived in Khartoum. I only half expected anyone would be there to meet me. I had memorized my instructions in case no one was--take a taxi to the Acropole Hotel and ask for George; he'll find you a room. It sounded like a line Humphrey Bogart might have delivered in the classic film *Casablanca*. Intrigued, I had envisioned myself arriving at 2:00 a.m. in a strange African city where I imagined everyone would be at least 6 feet 6 inches tall and black as the night. I expected George to be blacker and taller than everyone else, to be wearing a white *jallabia* and a red fez, and to be standing guard in front of the Acropole Hotel when I arrived in a rickety yellow taxi with my luggage piled on top. George, I found out the next day, was a Greek and part owner of the hotel.

I knew Sudan was going to be hotter than Egypt the instant I stepped off the plane. Midnight in Khartoum felt like noon in Cairo. Never in my life had I experienced anything as hot as the next afternoon in Khartoum. I had to spend two days there obtaining travel documents, introductory letters to the heads of the Sudanese Commissioner for Refugees in each of the camps where I'd be working, letters to the police chiefs of each of the towns where I'd be living, and verification of my nursing license. During the six months that followed, no one ever asked to see any of these papers or documents.

One of the main reasons the American Refugee Committee stationed Bob Medrala in Khartoum, hundreds of miles from the nearest refugee camp, was to meet new arrivals such as me, guide us through this bureaucratic process, and get us onto busses headed in the direction of the camps near Sudan's eastern border with Ethiopia. Otherwise, overwhelmed by the shock of the paralyzing heat, faced with the seemingly impossible task of finding the various government ministries scattered through several buildings along the Nile and then having to deal with the bureaucrats therein, some of us might have turned around and gone back home. The thought crossed my mind.

The furnace-like heat sapped me of everything, of every desire except thirst. It took my appetite, so that when I tried to eat I felt like vomiting. It took a conscious effort to turn my head to look out for cars when crossing a street. I wanted to get from one point to the next only by the shortest possible route. Once, I had to run halfway across a street to avoid being hit by a taxi. Immediately, I made a mental note to avoid running that far again at any time during the next six months. Until the week before, and for the previous several years, I had run 60 to 70 miles a week just for the fun of it. Now, suddenly, I was vowing not to run 60 feet if I could avoid it. I felt lightheaded and found it difficult to concentrate.

My initial culture shock was almost as bad as the heat shock. I was at once astounded and discouraged by the disinterest shown by the bureaucrats who were supposed to process my papers. One after another told Bob and me they couldn't have my papers ready until *bukkra,* tomorrow…*mumkin,* maybe. Before the end of the first day, I was fantasizing about ways to get out of Sudan and back home without great loss of face.

First I fantasized that it poured rain for a week, fields turned green and all the refugees went back to Ethiopia. (I didn't know at that point that the refugees were Eritreans, not Ethiopians). That would make all relief workers expendable and I would be sent home. Then I thought: Sudan could have another *coup d'etat,* just as had occurred a month earlier when President Gaafar Muhammed Nimeire was overthrown. If that could happen, the new government probably would expel all foreigners and the U.S. government would airlift me out by tomorrow, if not sooner. I liked the idea of immediate expulsion best; the sooner out of the heat, the better. If you're standing so close to a campfire that you're afraid your clothes might catch fire, which is what if felt like during the hottest part of the day, do you want to get away from the heat right now or wait two weeks?

I don't know how hot it was that first day in Khartoum. It was certainly more than 100 degrees, probably less than 200. Bob said it felt like about 115. "But it could get hotter," he said, matter-of-factly. I felt like if I stood in one place too long, my shoes would melt and weld me to the ground.

The heat was only the beginning of my miseries in Khartoum. It was so hot that I was thirsty whenever I wasn't asleep, but there was almost nothing suitable to drink. Water came out of the taps hot. I found no juice bars or tea shops in Khartoum. The bottled soft drinks were intolerably sweet. There was no beer in Sudan and hadn't been for years. The Muslim government had outlawed alcoholic beverages. I gulped down as much tea and ice water with fresh lime juice as I could each time we stopped at the Acropole Hotel, where Bob ate breakfast and lunch every day. Although I could only look nauseously at my food, I couldn't get enough to drink.

The heat was unbearable, my thirst unquenchable. I drank glass after glass of hot tap water at the house where I stayed in Khartoum. This was a house rented by two relief agencies—the American Refugee Committee and Lalmba Association. New arrivals such as me stayed there and vacationing relief workers slept there when they needed to get away from the camps for a few days. I wondered why anyone voluntarily, of his own free will, would come to Khartoum for a holiday. I tried not to imagine the relief workers' living conditions if this was where they came for rest and recreation.

I drank so much water that I'd gotten an around-the-clock sampling of Khartoum's water-borne microscopic wildlife and had developed profuse, explosive, unrelenting diarrhea before I'd been in Khartoum 24 hours. I became dangerously dehydrated so quickly that my tongue dried up, making me periodically unable to speak. Sometimes this happened within an hour of drinking so much that I couldn't hold another swallow. My urine output ceased. I was able to pee only about two ounces at a time, once or twice a day. Before that situation righted itself nearly a week later, I worried I might suffer serious and permanent kidney damage.

Bob, seeing how fast I was dehydrating, took me to the dispensary at the American Embassy. There, the nurse gave me a bottle of kaopectate to slow down the diarrhea, and several packets of oral rehydration solution—a powdered mixture of salt, sugar, potassium and bicarbonate of soda—to replace the electrolytes my body was losing. She made me swallow some kaopectate, a packet of ORS and as much filtered embassy water as I could hold before letting me back on the streets. Within an hour of leaving the embassy, though, I was again thirsty for a glass of Khartoum's hot bacteria- and amoeba-infested tap water. When your tongue becomes so dry you can't talk, you drink whatever is available and worry about the consequences later.

TWO

Although desperate to get out of Khartoum, I was nervous about leaving. I was headed for Kassala, a small city in eastern Sudan within sight of the Ethiopian border. Kassala was also less than 10 miles from Wad Sherife, a reception center that in the previous few months had absorbed approximately 70,000 refugees. It was still continuing to grow daily.

Most of my nervousness was about the eight-hour bus ride across the dessert and how I'd manage to stop the bus and get off with the onset of each attack of diarrhea. It's impossible to overstate the anxiety that goes with the raging diarrhea that can affect travelers to underdeveloped countries. This is not the kind of diarrhea you become aware of only after you've passed a stool and noticed it was loose or watery. This kind comes with a sudden overwhelming feeling that if you don't get your pants down right now, you'll have to change them. The feeling occurs five, maybe 10 times a day.

Bob took me by taxi to the bus at 6:00 in the morning. There was no bus station in Khartoum, or anywhere else in Sudan I would see during the next six months, even though busses were the most common means of long-distance public transportation. Cars were as common in Sudan as cool days.

The taxi driver took us to a large, dusty, unpaved area on the edge of the city where a fleet of busses were parked helter-skelter. No two busses looked like they belonged to the same company. There was a red one, a yellow one, a red and yellow one, a blue one, a green one, a pink and blue one, a green and white one, more than 20 in all. Each was painted and decorated, apparently, to suit the tastes of the individual owner. This was private enterprise on a small scale, not some Sudanese Greyhound.

Bob had bought my ticket the previous evening although there appeared no risk I'd be unable to get a seat on the morning of departure. As soon as we opened the door to get out of the taxi, we were besieged by a horde of boys and young men. Half of them wanted to sell us bus tickets while the other half were intent on taking my luggage. In the midst of such apparent chaos, with everyone pushing and trying to out shout everyone else to get our attention, I visualized my four pieces of luggage going off in four different directions.

The largest piece was a battered simulated-leather suitcase that had been in the family at least three generations. This relic, which had traveled in Africa a good 25 years before I ever had, could no longer be securely locked. In fact, it had to be wrapped this way and that with several yards of good strong clothesline. This not only kept it from popping open, it kept it from disintegrating altogether. Unfortunately, I was making this particular journey with the case secured only with a dozen or so yards of heavy jute cord. I had used the clothesline to tie up two other pieces of luggage—a cardboard box that contained several of the textbooks I'd be using for the classes I'd be teaching, and a portable typewriter, sandwiched between two three-inch thick pieces of foam cushioning. I hoped the foam cushions would protect the typewriter until I got to Kassala and later serve as seat cushions when traveling by four-wheel drive vehicle across roadless parts of the desert. I also carried a small backpack that contained the most valuable of my possessions.

The red and yellow bus on which Bob had bought my ticket was a typical Third World bus. Baggage was stacked on the roof and people were packed inside. There was no load limit. There were five adults and four children in the five seats in my row in the bus. Once all the seats had been filled, the driver and his assistant began filling the center aisle with the luggage that wouldn't fit on the roof. This created a whole new set of perches for passengers who didn't have seats.

We left Khartoum at 7:00 a.m. sharp. Almost all inter-city busses in Sudan start out between 6:00 and 7:00 a.m. to beat the heat, so to speak. You never really beat it, but traveling when it's hot (morning) was preferable to when it was hotter (midday) and hottest (afternoon).

I had decided to eat nothing and drink little before leaving to help prevent diarrhea. For breakfast, I had two swallows of kaopectate and a glass of oral rehydration solution.

At 9:30 the bus made its first stop, pulling off the two-lane road to park on the edge of a "defecation site." There, almost everybody got off and spread out into the desert until he or she found a bush to squat behind. My stool was bright yellow and loose but not watery. I had managed not to humiliate myself by shitting in my pants. I'd realized once the aisles of the bus had been packed with baggage and people that there was no hope of asking the driver to make any unscheduled stops on my behalf. I couldn't have gotten from my seat, next to the window halfway back the bus on the right, to the driver, if my life had depended on it. And if I had been able to, what could I have told the driver? I didn't speak Arabic. I doubted that he spoke English. I cringed at the thought of climbing over row after row of people in the aisle to reach the driver, and then, in the front of the bus as we rolled across the desert at 60 miles an hour, having to do a pantomime of why I needed to get off.

When we got back on the bus after the first stop, I took half a dozen swallows from my water bottle. I had been warned never to travel any distance, anywhere in Sudan, without a water bottle. There would be days later when I would look back on that as life-saving advice. I never ignored it.

There was, in fact, water provided for the bus passengers. A bucket of water and an aluminum cup were passed through the bus every 90 minutes or so by the driver's assistant. They were passed from person to person, the one bucket and one cup, until everyone with a thirst had shared and drank from the single aluminum cup. I was scared to take the risk. I wasn't anxious to get hepatitis my first week away from home.

At 12:30 we made another stop at another defecation site, next to a cluster of roadside *recubbas* or shelters selling coffee, tea, bread, beans and grilled goat meat. I had become so dried up I didn't even need to look for a bush. Instead, I drank the rest of my quart bottle of water. Then, for one Sudanese pound, about 30 cents, I bought a watermelon from an old man squatting on the ground between a pile of melons and his camel, which was eating discarded watermelon rinds. This would be the only thing I'd eat all day. The watermelon was as hot as the weather, surely over 100 degrees, but I consumed about two-thirds of it with great relish in less than five minutes. I gave the rest to a woman and her four children who were sitting opposite me in the bus.

My fear of diarrhea hadn't been my only fear as I got on the bus that morning. I wished I'd had enough clothesline to tie my suitcase closed instead of having used jute cord. I couldn't help imagining the whole thing bursting apart while being loaded or unloaded, and most of the belongings I'd need during the next six months being scattered across the desert. Ever more worrisome was my backpack, which I hand-held or kept under my feet during every minute of the bus ride. It contained 340 tubes of tetracycline eye ointment and more than 15,000 Sudanese pounds (the equivalent of $5,000 cash) that I was delivering from Bob to the field in Kassala. This was operating expense money for the refugee camp at Wad Sherife for the next several weeks.

Furthermore, I was the only white person on the bus and undoubtedly the only passenger who didn't speak Arabic. This was particularly significant because we were traveling eight hours across the desert to a town I might not recognize on arrival since I wouldn't be able to read the signs written in Arabic script when we got there.

Plus, there probably wouldn't be anybody to meet me when I got to Kassala either, Bob said. "They'll all be working at Wad Sherife. God only knows when the bus will arrive, anyway." He instructed me to ask a taxi driver to take me to the Swiss Red Cross because he probably won't have heard of Lalmba or the American Refugee Committee. The Swiss would put me in touch with them, he said. Bob apologized for being unable to give me the addresses of any of the three organizations, explaining that they didn't have any. The unpaved streets of Kassala were neither named nor numbered, so in effect, everybody lived at an unlisted address.

As we shook hands and I got on the bus to leave Khartoum, Bob gave me my final instructions: "Make sure you don't lose the money."

THREE

I had been preparing myself to work in a refugee camp for four months, but until four weeks before I arrived at one I hadn't known where it would be. I didn't know whether I'd be working with Afghan refugees in Pakistan, Cambodians in Thailand, Eritreans in Sudan, or with someone else in a part of the world where I hadn't even known there was a need.

Now, as I rode across the barren stretch of desert between Kassala and Wad Sherife in the front seat of a four-wheel drive Toyota Land Cruiser, I suddenly felt inadequate and totally unprepared for the experience ahead. I had seen photographs, television programs and videos about the refugees from Eritrea. I had read all the daily newspaper and magazine articles about refugees and several books that I thought would help prepare me. Earlier in my life, I had spent more than six months traveling through the poorest Third World countries, from Afghanistan to Indonesia, which should have immunized me against culture shock anywhere. Once I had agreed to join the combined Lalmba Association-American Refugee Committee team in Sudan, where I would teach health care to refugees from Eritrea, I had talked to everyone I could find who had done similar work. Still, I hadn't a hint of what I'd feel at the first sight of a refugee camp.

I came prepared to be emotionally devastated. At the same time, I hoped I wouldn't be. I asked myself if I'd see anything as disturbing as some of the sights I'd seen in India 17 years earlier.

The single most powerful and lasting image of my life had been of a naked baby, sitting alone in the middle of a defecation area on the broiling hot pavement outside the Howrah Railway Station in Calcutta. The temperature was at least 110 degrees. The rank odor of feces and urine was overpowering. The baby had diarrhea and was covered with flies. Its mother was nowhere in sight. I could still visualize that abandoned, naked, fly-covered baby and recall the horror I felt that day so many years before.

I suffered an emotional knockout then. I couldn't walk past that area again during my remaining days in Calcutta. I half expected to see similarly shocking sights at Wad Sherife. I hoped I'd be mature enough now to react by wanting to help rather than run away.

My anxiety was all for naught. Amazingly, my first day at Wad Sherife was one of the most joyous of my life. I was totally inspired to see what was being done. There were volunteers from Australia, Belgium, Canada, England, Eritrea, Germany, Ireland, Norway, Scotland, Sudan, Switzerland and the United States, working together in perfect harmony. Their supplies were limited but I saw food that had come from Denmark and Japan, medicines from China and Finland. My spirit was uplifted to see so many people who had come so far from so many countries to work together, sometimes with little other than their compassion and resourcefulness, in the common cause of helping those in such desperate need.

I would find later that the many international relief agencies would work together in a spirit of cooperation, sharing and harmony incomprehensible to anyone accustomed to the competitive ways of the modern industrialized world. I had never seen so many people giving so much, truly giving from their hearts, while asking absolutely nothing in return. I felt for the first time in my life part of a true brotherhood of man.

I spent my first day being guided around the camp, a sprawling collection of huts and shacks, or *tukuls* and *recubbas*, built almost entirely of crude forked poles and hand-woven palm mats. Every building had a dirt floor. Almost none was as tall as seven feet. Each had been constructed by hand in the truest sense of the words since almost no tools were available.

Three-inch diameter poles placed upright into holes in the ground formed the perimeter of each structure. Typically, a man squatted on the ground and used a short piece of steel rod as a tool to dig a hole through the hard crust of the desert floor. Then, he scooped the loose soil out of each hole, one handful at a time. He repeated the process over and over until the holes were deep enough to support the poles. Additional poles were tied crossways with rope to the upright poles to complete the frame of each house.

Mats were fastened to the frames with wire. If you wanted a window, you took a knife and cut a hole through the mat wall. The upright poles were Y-shaped at the top. These forks supported poles laid crossways, which supported mats that formed the roofs.

The same simple materials and construction methods had been used to build everything from the smallest refugee *tukul* I saw, covering barely 15 square feet of ground, to the LARC (Lalmba-American Refugee Committee) hospital, which contained about 30 beds. Many of the beds had been made by hand of similar materials. By a truly ingenious procedure, crude poles were carved and fitted together to form a frame. Then a long piece of rope was strung tightly back and forth from end-to-end and side-to-side again and again to hold the frame together. This formed a surprisingly comfortable and sometimes aesthetically beautiful bed. A palm mat was sometimes used as a mattress, although it was not unusual for people to sleep directly on the ropes.

Each refugee family had been provided with poles and mats with which to put up its *tukul*. Some were constructed much more cleverly than others. Some were shaped like miniature A-frames, others looked like boxes, still others like cross-sections of domes or a quarter of a grapefruit. I surmised that the different shapes represented different tribal backgrounds. In some cases, though, the difference between one *tukul* and another clearly was just a matter of one builder having more imagination and being more clever with his hands than another.

However they were built, the *tukuls* were all pitifully small when you considered that people were living in them, not on overnight camping trips. Some were the size of pup tents. Some Americans have larger closets. I was taken into one and was amazed to find a man, a woman, seven children and a calf inside. I was amused to see a goat tethered to the outside of another. A goat can eat just about anything on earth except glass, rocks and razor blades. This one was eating the *tukul* to which he was tethered.

The creativity of the refugees touched me deeply. It was amazing to see how much individuality they had put into their *tukuls* when they had so little to work with. Belongings were hung from stubs of branches on the poles that supported the walls. There were a variety of cooking pits and fireplaces, made from dried mud and in some cases a stone or two. Human creativity apparently has no limits when one is faced with the necessity to survive.

Many of these *tukuls*, which by anybody's standards were pitiful excuses for homes, had been given a warm and homey feeling. It was a bittersweet experience to see them. One part of me wanted to cry in sadness, another part in the joy of seeing what a human being can do to survive when his back is to the wall.

The LARC half of the camp at Wad Sherife was divided into several sections. Strategically located throughout were feeding centers, outpatient clinics, a dispensary, food warehouses, a clothing and blanket distribution center, and the inpatient hospital. The Swiss Red Cross half of the camp was similar. Everything was built of the same simple materials—poles and mats, rope and wire—with two exceptions. The Swiss used a large army tent as a warehouse. Their medical clinic was made of mud bricks, topped with a thatched straw roof.

Everything looked the same from a distance. From within, the camp seemed to reach out to the horizon in every direction. Immense as it was, the whole camp looked like it could be blown away by one good gust of wind. I would find later that these structures were wind resistant in their own unique way. The wind, and the heavy clouds of dust it carried, simply blew right through them, going in one side and out the other. It was much cooler inside the mat-and-pole *tukuls* than inside the only canvas tent I went into.

Everywhere I went I saw smiling faces and was greeted by people calling out *"khawaja!"* Foreigner! It seemed like every single child at Wad Sherife reached out to touch my hand as I passed. The children made me feel like some great pop star, or Santa Claus. I had my hand out and a smile on my face all day long. An old man clasped my outstretched hand in both of his and said humbly in perhaps the only English words he knew: "Thank you."

I couldn't get over how happy most of the refugees looked. I wondered what they were so happy about. They looked happy even when dressed in rags that barely fit within the definition of clothing. Many of the refugees were idle, but at least as many were busy at one thing or another. Men helped one another build their *tukuls*. Women squatted on the ground as they prepared food over tiny charcoal fires. A good number of refugees were actually employed by LARC and the Swiss Red Cross as health care workers, builders, cooks in the feeding centers, storekeepers in the storage huts, and registrars and clerks in the food, clothing and blanket distribution centers. An artist was working as a sign painter. Sadly, several men also worked as gravediggers.

Surprisingly few people appeared to be starving, except those in the inpatient and outpatient clinics and in the feeding centers. No one appeared to be an ounce overweight either.

Perhaps I'd been naïve to expect everyone to have the look of hopelessness and near starvation that much of the world had seen so many times on television and in newspaper and magazine photographs. I should have known, being a former journalist, that the media would dwell on the underside of the story, focus on the most miserable of the suffering thousands. My cynicism was tempered by the understanding that if the media hadn't dramatized the famine and mass exodus of refugees from Eritrea, there wouldn't have been the moving sympathetic worldwide response. For once, the media had done a great service in its sensationalism of a tragic situation. I was glad. I might not have been there otherwise.

21

FOUR

A newspaper article on January 14, 1985, triggered my going to Sudan. The San Francisco *Chronicle* printed a short wire service story about volunteer nurses arriving in Ethiopia. I remember the date because it was my 46th birthday. My wife Margaret read me the story aloud and asked: "Wouldn't you like to do something like that?" Something in the way she asked made me think she was offering me the opportunity to go, giving me permission, rather than just tossing out an idea to test my reaction.

"I'd love to," I said without hesitation. "But I don't think I could just go off and leave you with the children. Anyway, if I was going to do something like that, I'd rather go to Pakistan."

For years I'd had a soft spot in my heart for the Afghan refugees in Pakistan. In fact, for the previous several months I'd been trying to figure out a way to gather up the worn out running shoes collecting dust in the closets of the tens of thousands of runners and joggers in the United States. I wanted to send them off to Pakistan. I had several pairs myself, no longer good enough to absorb the shock of running several miles a day but plenty good to cover the bare feet of refugees. Thousands of Afghan families had been forced to flee their homes, leaving behind their possessions, to resettle in Pakistan following the bombing and invasion of their country by the Soviet Union.

I also had contemplated sending a small amount of money to the International Rescue Committee, which I had read was doing good work helping the Afghan refugees. I was hesitant to send money though, until I could be reasonably certain it would help. I was awaiting a reply to a letter I'd sent to IRC, asking for details about their work.

It didn't take long for Margaret and I to convince one another that she was sincere in offering to let me go half way around the world and that I was sincere about wanting to go. The next morning, I phoned the local office of the Red Cross to find out how I could volunteer. I was told the American Red Cross rarely sends people abroad, but was given the names and addresses of three organizations which might: IRC, International Voluntary Services and Amdoc Option Agency. I immediately wrote to all three, telling each I was anxious to volunteer my help.

Having done that, I decided I should find out if I could get time off from my job at the hospital where I had been working seven years as a nurse, taking care of cancer patients. I was told I could take six months unpaid leave of absence and that I'd need to give two weeks notice before leaving. I fully expected to be on my way in about three weeks, by early February. I expected IRC, IVS and Amdoc to phone me the moment they received my letters. I thought that if I volunteered for something, especially to work in some undesirable part of the world, I would have people competing with one another for my services. That was a naïve assumption.

Amdoc wrote back to say they were a matchmaker agency for volunteers and small low-profile relief organizations. They sent me an application to fill out and a list of jobs currently available worldwide. They said they'd contact me when something came along for which I appeared qualified.

I also received postal replies rather than urgent phone calls from IRC and IVS, both of which came without job offers. By then I had found the names of a number of other relief organizations, and in turn I wrote to each. Some wrote back saying they needed only volunteers with previous Third World experience. Some wanted a year's commitment. Some provided developmental aid but did not send medical people. Some said they'd gladly accept a monetary donation but didn't want me. Very few were doing anything in Pakistan.

The night Margaret and I saw the film *The Killing Fields*, I decided I didn't necessarily have to go to Pakistan. I was so moved by the final scenes in which Dith Pran escaped from Cambodia and arrived at a refugee camp in Thailand that I wanted to work with refugees anywhere, the sooner the better.

My letters volunteering myself to different organizations continued and so did the negative responses. I wrote to and was turned down by The End Hunger Network, International Rescue Committee, Unitarian Universalist Service Committee, The Billings Clinic, World Vision, Catholic Relief Services, Amigos de las Americas, The Hesperian Foundation, Direct Relief International, Christian Medical Society, American Red Cross, Project Concern International, National Council of Churches of Christ, InterAction, Project Hope, CARE, Oxfam America, International Voluntary Services and the TransCentury Recruitment Center.

Each gave a seemingly valid reason for turning me down and I didn't lost hope. I was disappointed though, when February passed and then March, and I still hadn't found anyone who would let me give them six months of my time. I was particularly disappointed when the relief agency with its headquarters nearest my home, Medical Volunteers International, didn't even answer my letter. I had read an article in the San Francisco *Chronicle* about MVI doctors and nurses departing the San Francisco Bay Area for Sudan. I found their phone number, called and was told to write, stating my wishes and qualifications. I never heard back.

Finally, I received a letter dated April 12, from Marty Downey of Lalmba Association in Golden, Colorado. Lalmba had heard about me through Amdoc, the matchmaker agency to which I had written before almost anyone else, in January.

> Dear Richard,
>   It has recently been brought to our attention that you are interested in locating in a position overseas, perhaps a

Third World Country. Please find enclosed some general information regarding Lalmba Association…who we are and how we came to be working in E. Africa. We hope you will enjoy reading the material!

Hugh & I just returned after spending 3 weeks in the Sudan along the Ethiopian border where our medical clinics are situated. We had been urged by our staff there to visit and to see for ourselves the drastic changes which have occurred since our last visit there just last fall! We were simply amazed to see hundreds of thousands of poor famine victims massed together into new refugee areas! And the refugees continue to come. We were asked by the United Nations High Commissioner for Refugees and the Sudan Commissioner for Refugees in Dec. to take over a 4th refugee settlement (the other three we have been working in for 5 years now). In a telex received to today we learned that the refugee camp we took in Dec. which numbered 5,000 at the time is presently up to 12,000! And we are being asked to still do more though we have increased our American medical personnel from 8 to 16 this past month! (We have approximately 120 African staff).

Probably you haven't heard of Lalmba before. We are a small but a very effective relief organization and we have been working in E. Africa for more than 20 years now. We are very committed to helping these poor, sick starving people in East Africa. We are in need of physicians, nurses and allied medical personnel to help replace physicians, etc. currently there…the sooner the better! If interested, we hope that you will contact us soon. Please feel free to call either Hugh or I collect at the number listed at the top of this letter to let us help you answer questions, concerns, etc. We hope to hear from you in the near future!

Very Sincerely,
Marty Downey

I phoned as soon as I finished reading the letter. Lalmba wanted someone to teach health care to refugees in Sudan. I didn't know if I was qualified. I had worked as a nurse for 13 years but had done no formal teaching. I said I'd have to think about it.

Lalmba's history of aiding Africans dated back more than 30 years. Hugh Downey, a soldier from Kansas City, had been shocked by the poverty, hunger and suffering he saw while stationed in Eritrea in 1962. He became obsessed with the idea of helping. After discharge, he married his childhood sweetheart, Marty Meagher. In 1965, they went to Eritrea to begin a commitment that since has only deepened.

Lalmba is an Ethiopian word meaning Place of Hope. Hugh and Marty created one. In just 10 years, Lalmba established a 75-bed hospital, an orphanage for more than 100 children, a library, an obstetrics clinic and 10 village schools. Wells were dug, roads built, teachers trained and a prosthetics workshop begun. All this was accomplished in the midst of a civil war between Eritrea and Ethiopia. At one point, Marty was wounded in both legs by machine gun fire.

In 1977, all of Lalmba's properties and buildings were seized and nationalized by Ethiopia's Marxist government. The programs that had helped so many were forced to shut down. The orphanage became a barracks for Ethiopian soldiers.

However, when thousands of Eritreans crossed the border into eastern Sudan to escape the civil war, Lalmba followed right along. With the blessings of the Sudanese government, they resumed providing services there. The needs were greater than ever. I was excited that Hugh and Marty thought I could help.

After working all night at the hospital, I returned home at 8:30 in the morning to be told by Margaret that I had just missed a phone call from Marty. I returned her call. She asked if I could be in Colorado the next day for an interview and orientation. She said a pre-paid ticket would be at the airport for me, if I said yes. I said yes.

Suddenly, I was caught in a whirlwind of activity after wondering for three months if I'd ever get a positive response to one of my letters.

Marty met me at the Denver airport at noon the next day. We chatted for half an hour while we waited for Alan Lefkowitz, a doctor from Connecticut, who was also flying in for an interview and orientation. Then, she took us both to their home where she and Hugh fed us, gave us stacks of papers to read, showed us videos of Lalmba's team at work in Sudan, and answered questions. They then signed me to an agreement which said, basically, that I would work for six months without pay in a very poor country in very hot weather and that I would have to pay only an $800 portion of my airfare to get there. I was thrilled to have gotten such a good deal. Alan wasn't ready to make a commitment, although he eventually would.

Before taking me to the airport the next day, Hugh explained that I would be spending part of my time working with a combined group of Lalmba and American Refugee Committee workers. ARC was a relief agency that had operated refugee camps in Thailand but had done no previous work in Africa. When a number of ARC volunteers expressed interest in helping in Sudan, they were referred to Lalmba, which brought them under its umbrella. ARC paid the expenses of its volunteers, creating a temporary amalgamation of the two agencies. It was the first evidence I'd see of the extraordinary cooperation that existed, both between individuals and their organizations, in the famine relief effort.

FIVE

At age 46, I was the oldest Lalmba-ARC volunteer in Sudan. I didn't mind—46, 57, 68, whatever; it didn't matter. Each additional year just meant more experience, more knowledge, more wisdom. Theoretically.

After a week in Kassala, theory went out the window. I had gotten a week older, but dumber, not wiser. I descended to the depths of stupidity by going for a run in the midday sun. I became so hot and dehydrated so rapidly, I actually thought I might die. I felt like I was turning into jerky.

I had run regularly in California at a pace of less than seven minutes a mile in 60-degree temperatures. The day I arrived in Kassala, I found a running partner in Vic Snyder, who was a slower runner but such good company that I gladly slowed my pace to be able to run with him at sunrise each morning.

Vic was one of several truly remarkable people I would meet in Sudan. He was a physician who had worked previously as a volunteer in Sierra Leone, Thailand and Honduras. In the United States, he sheltered Cuban refugees in his home. As a college student, he took a summer job as a nurse's aide in a nursing home for the aged. He had left his practice in Little Rock, where his patients included the inmates of the Arkansas State Penitentiary, to spend three months in Sudan. He entertained thoughts of going to law school when he returned home, as a possible avenue into politics. He felt that as an elected public servant he might ultimately be able to do the most good for the most people.

Despite this impressive background and his noble ideals, Dr. Vic Snyder was in other ways an absolutely ordinary guy. He could awaken from a night's sleep and say something funny before he even put his feet on the floor. He could crack the tension during the most difficult times at work with some witty insight that had just flashed across his mind. Most members of the LARC team considered him our Hawkeye, in reference to the comical and spiritual leader of the old television show *M*A*S*H.*

Another thing about Vic: he had common sense. He recognized his limits. During the African spring, even at 5:15 in the morning, running four miles at nine minutes per mile gave him the exercise he wanted but didn't impair his ability to function during the rest of the day. Being faster and accustomed to running more miles per week than Vic, I thought I could easily run farther and faster any time I felt like it. I decided this only a week after telling myself in Khartoum that I didn't want to run across the street again in such heat. Now I'd decided to run eight or nine miles on my first day off. I decided to do it in the daytime instead of at dawn so I wouldn't have to get up at 5:15.

I hydrated myself well before starting, taking in as much water as I could hold. I put on a white cap to reflect the sun off my head. I wore my running shoes, shorts, no shirt, and I soaked a bandana in cold water and tied it around my neck. Then I started out over the same route that Vic and I covered quite easily each morning. The route followed a path along the levee bordering the dry bed of the River Gash. The river had disappeared during the drought, although it eventually would reappear with the coming of the rains in Ethiopia, where the Gash originated.

I started running, I guessed, at about 7½ minutes per mile. I thought I'd run 30 minutes away from home and then turn back. I was even thinking that if I felt good enough, I might do another out-and-back in the opposite direction. I carried a quart container of water in each hand and promised myself I'd stop to drink after 30 minutes, thirsty or not, to keep from getting dehydrated.

I don't know exactly how hot it was that day. People who had wall thermometers in Sudan kept them in the shade because the scale on them went only to 120 degrees. The mercury often reached the top, even in the shade. I had foolishly chosen to run in the direct sun.

Twelve minutes after starting, I felt like I'd run into the wall of a burning building. I slowed to a walk and tried to drink. I couldn't walk, drink and breathe at the same time. I came to a dead halt, caught my breath and drank half a quart of water, which already had turned warm. When I started to run again, I realized immediately I would be unable to resume my 7:30 per mile pace.

I had been out about 20 minutes by the time I made my second water stop. By then I was nearing the end of the levee. The levee turned right, then left at a dried up donkey carcass, and then just disappeared altogether so that the riverbed and desert merged and looked like one and the same.

I was already beginning to realize that running 30 minutes away from home might be a little risky, like swimming too far out from shore. I was starting to get lightheaded, was slowing down and feeling like I'd stayed too long in a sauna. My brain was simmering. I could no longer remember exactly when I'd started, so I turned back for home.

Almost immediately after turning back, I met a young man in a dazzling white *jallabia,* the long flowing cotton gown worn by most Sudanese men. He motioned me to stop, which I did. I offered him a drink from the one water bottle that I hadn't yet drained. He held it up to his nose, sniffed it disapprovingly, pointed to my wristwatch and indicated: "No thanks, I don't want your smelly water. I'll take your watch." His gesture wasn't one of "can I have it?" but rather of "I *will* take that."

We carried on a brief pantomime since neither of us spoke the other's language. He kept indicating he wanted my watch. I feigned ignorance and tried to get him to drink my water. I pretended I hadn't noticed he wanted my watch. I couldn't pretend I didn't see the thick hardwood walking stick at his side. I hoped he wouldn't decide to use it as a weapon. When he indicated he wanted to look in the pocket of my running shorts, I was happy to show him it was empty.

Deciding it was time to break the stalemate and put some distance between the two of us, I gestured that I wanted my water bottle back if he wasn't going to drink. He gestured he'd trade it for my watch. I held out the screw top for the bottle. Surprisingly, he handed me the bottle. I replaced the top, said in Arabic *ma 'a salaama*, peace be with you, and then suddenly turned and took off running across the desert, headed for home.

He came after me, calling out unintelligibly in Arabic. But in his sandals and *jallabia*, he couldn't close the gap I had put between us with my initial burst of speed. He chased me for several minutes but when I got back to the intersection of the desert, the dried donkey and the levee, I met two people coming the other way. At the sight of them, he stopped calling to me and gave up the chase.

By then the heat had seriously weakened me. I felt so hot I fantasized my running shorts might burst spontaneously into flames. My pace slowed to probably slower than 10 minutes per mile. I was well into my second quart of water. The heat was searing my lungs, making me cough and forcing me to stop and walk periodically to catch my breath. By the last half mile I was able to jog slowly for only about 200 yards at a time, with walking interludes of about 50 yards.

The total elapsed time from departure to my return home was about 45 minutes. I had spent at least five minutes of that time walking or standing still. I had drunk two quarts of water and had covered at most five miles. I could barely stand. I had the running-on-empty feeling that marathon runners sometimes feel at the end of their run if they've gone too fast over the first 20 miles of their 26-mile race.

During my remaining 5½ months in Sudan, I would never again begin a run after 5:30 a.m.

SIX

Like Dr. Vic Snyder, Susan Smith was a person who possessed an extraordinary amount of compassion for the underprivileged of the world. A nurse practitioner from Alberta, she had worked previously helping Inuits in Canada's remote Northwest Territories above the Arctic Circle, had been part of the American Refugee Committee's relief effort during the exodus of refugees from Cambodia, and had done previous volunteer work in Africa in Botswana.

Now she brought her experience, her deep sense of caring and her boundless energy to Wad Sherife, where she was medical director of the Lalmba-American Refugee Committee (LARC) program. She effervesced with a contagious positive energy as she went about her work. No job was too big or too small for her. In a single day she might spend time performing mundane clerical tasks, making heart-rending personnel decisions or complicated judgments about future supply needs, or doing just plain hard physical work under the scorching African sun. There appeared to be no limits to the number and variety of jobs she could do, nor to the weight of responsibility she could bear.

Within two weeks of my arrival at Wad Sherife there was an outbreak of cholera, a highly contagious disease that can spread like wildfire and kill previously unaffected victims virtually overnight. It was quite conceivable that the whole camp of 70,000, whose general health and resistance was already poor due to malnutrition, could be wiped out by a cholera epidemic.

To avoid such a catastrophe, policies had to be created where none previously existed. An enormous number of critical decisions had to be made within a period of a few days. Susan and Swiss Red Cross medical director Dr. Joe Carragher decided at the onset that LARC and SRC should work as partners in a cooperative effort. Together they could ensure an immediate and ongoing sharing of knowledge and experience and avoid any waste or money or manpower in duplication of services. By joining forces, we would maximize the supplies of intravenous fluids and medications as well as the contacts for getting more supplies that, in such dire emergency, we might need to obtain overnight.

From the moment of the decision to combine forces with the Swiss, Susan worked tirelessly, participating with them and our own people in making one critical decision after another.

Some decisions were purely medical, such as approving a treatment protocol stating how many milligrams of tetracycline an adult cholera patient should receive per dose, how many doses should be given per day, and for how many days. On the surface, it would appear that arriving at such decisions would be simple. Recommended doses, intervals between doses and total length of treatment were clearly stated in any number of medical and pharmacology books and in a protocol circulated to all relief agencies in Sudan by UNHCR (United Nations High Commission for Refugees). However, there was often some philosophical issue to complicate the decision Susan had to make.

In this case, the issue was whether to give prophylactic treatment to pregnant women who had been in contact with those actually infected by cholera, knowing full well that giving tetracycline could damage the growing fetus but withholding it would put its mother at greater risk.

The boldest decision for which Susan had to shoulder

responsibility was to build a large cholera isolation hospital on the edge of camp. Fortunately, she was backed fully by project directors John Benson and Tom and Marissa Rogers.

There was no time to contact ARC headquarters in Minneapolis for permission, even though going ahead with the project would mean exceeding the entire year's construction budget before the year was half over. Communication systems in Sudan were so primitive that it might have taken two weeks to get word to Minneapolis and receive an answer.

The only public telephone in Kassala was at the post office. Just about every time one of us had tried to use it, we were told, "The lines are down. Try again tomorrow." The next day, we were told the same thing, "the lines are down. Try again tomorrow." I never once heard a phone ring during my time in Sudan. Mail service was also sporadic. I don't recall seeing or hearing a single plane in Sudan except at the airport in Khartoum. Airmail was a euphemism that didn't apply to us.

A decision on a cholera hospital had to be made now. Hundreds and perhaps thousands of cholera patients needed to be isolated from the refugee population, as soon as each was diagnosed. An isolation hospital had to be built immediately, not in two weeks or a month.

Still, before we could proceed, permission had to be obtained from Mohammed Osman, head of the Sudan Commission for Refugees at Wad Sherife. Osman had to approve all major decisions concerning refugees at Wad Sherife. He could be a formidable roadblock. There was concern he might not approve an isolation hospital. Approval would acknowledge there was a cholera outbreak, a fact the Sudanese government denied. There might be some gastroenteritis going around, the government said, but no cholera. Acknowledgement of a cholera epidemic might prompt the rest of the world to quarantine Sudan.

Mohammed Osman offered little resistance when Susan presented her plan to him. While he paid lip service to the official government position, he had such a fear of getting cholera himself that he would not even shake hands with refugees, lest he contact it from them.

The thought of designing a hospital in a week, to say nothing of building one, is mind-boggling if not downright laughable, when viewed from a western perspective.

Susan Smith and Carolyn Smith—no relation, but a remarkable person in her own right—decided the hospital should be built midway between the SRC and LARC hospitals on a piece of ground that refugee boys had cleared of rocks and feces to form a soccer field. Susan scribbled a plan on a scrap of paper, with outlines of a reception and screening area, acute and convalescent wards, a kitchen, latrines and a storage tent. This, she remembers, was one of the most difficult things she had to do at Wad Sherife. No one there had ever seen an isolation hospital before.

She and Carolyn used a stick to mark out the boundaries and floor plan of the hospital on the ground. Then the work began.

Carolyn quickly hired a crew of refugee builders. Together, they decided what materials would be needed to construct the hospital: how many poles, how many 4-by-12-foot mats, how much wire and rope. Someone was dispatched to Kassala to find the materials, barter over the price and get them delivered.

Susan decided how many latrines were needed and where they should be placed. Carolyn found refugees to dig them. Susan decided how many beds were needed for the hospital and she and Carolyn went about procuring them. Some came from other relief agencies, some from other refugee camps, some from the market in Kassala. Likewise, hundreds of plastic buckets had to be found for catching and containing vomit and diarrhea stools, the byproducts of cholera.

Since the hospital was a joint SRC-LARC venture, Susan and Joe Carragher worked together to hire staff, drawing equally from both sectors of the camp. They had to find and hire cooks, cleaners, registrars, guards and medical assistants. There was no shortage of applicants for the jobs, which paid about $40 per month. On the contrary, people practically begged to be hired. It was difficult turning many of them away.

Susan remembers interviewing a man named Andremarian, but turning him down because he had no dependents to support. She had to face him a second time when he returned to reapply, tears rolling down his cheeks, and pleaded to her: "I just want a job. All I want is a job."

"Are you hungry?" she asked him.

"I ate two days ago."

"Okay, then go join the other workers at lunch and come back tomorrow to the new hospital," Susan said, giving in. "You're hired."

The idea of the isolation hospital was conceived and approved; the hospital was designed, built and equipped, with 70 beds and space for an additional hundreds of patients on mats on the ground; and then it was staffed and became operational in the incredibly short period of 10 days. The next problem was getting people to use it. Refugees were dying of cholera in their *tukuls*, often at night, without having sought treatment.

Susan attacked this problem by giving a crash course in cholera prevention and recognition to the team of refugee home visitors. She then organized them to work around the clock to pass on the teaching to every family in the camp. The home visitors diagnosed many cases themselves, some while making their rounds by flashlight at night. Ultimately, they were responsible for saving the lives of countless others who they taught to seek treatment at the earliest detection of cholera symptoms.

One of Susan's strengths as medical director was that she was not afraid to delegate important jobs. She didn't try to do everything herself. She taught the home visitors about cholera prevention and the importance of early treatment, but left it to them to disseminate the information to everyone else in camp. She decided a cholera isolation hospital had to be built and even designed it, but turned over the task of getting it built to Carolyn.

And she decided my brief would be to educate the refugee health care workers so they could diagnose and treat their fellow refugees at such a level of proficiency that expatriate help could be phased out. In other words, I was to help make them independent in their health care.

She gave me several medical books, a list of names of refugees who would be my students and said I could have 2½ weeks to get ready for the first class. She then delegated the whole educational project to me. Anytime I wanted help or advice, all I had to do was ask her. But basically, she put the ball in my hands.

SEVEN

Two and a half weeks didn't seem like much time to prepare a course that was supposed to teach the refugees to become independent in their health care. But we didn't have any illusions. I wasn't founding a medical school. Nobody would be able to immigrate to the United States and get a job at the Mayo Clinic after completing the course. I'd just do the best I could.

I didn't have the faintest idea how long the course would last. I had only a sketchy idea in my head of what the course content would be, no detailed plan. I didn't know how much the students already knew or what they needed to learn. I didn't know how well they spoke English, how fast I'd be able to go through my lessons, whether I'd need to repeat everything twice, or if I'd have to write every word of every lesson on a chalkboard. I had never stood in front of a group and taught a class in my life.

I also knew next to nothing about tropical medicine, although I knew I would have to devote important segments of the course to such diseases as malaria, tuberculosis and cholera. Although I had been a nurse for 13 years, my only preparation for teaching this class before arriving in Sudan was to have read one book, *Where There Is No Doctor;* part of another, *Helping Health Care Workers Learn;*

38

and a magazine article about malaria I found on the airplane coming over. I found it in the pocket on the back of the seat in front of me, tucked in behind the vomit bag. I didn't remember anything I read in the article except that malaria had killed more people than all the wars in history combined and that you get it from being bitten by female mosquitoes. Males eat only fruit.

Another thing: there wasn't a classroom at Wad Sherife; there were few textbooks, fewer visual aids and no desks.

Susan had anticipated many of these problems and needs weeks before my arrival. The concept of teaching the refugees to become independent in their health care had been described in a grant request, sent to the Dutch government, which had responded by giving approximately $5,000 to the project. That would be more than enough to finance construction of a classroom out of local building materials and to furnish and equip it with desks and benches, a chalkboard and chalk, a storage cupboard, notebooks, paper and pens.

The remainder of the grant could be used to pay the salaries of the students, about $45 per month. The students would receive six to eight hours of classroom instruction per week and work fulltime as medical assistants in the inpatient and outpatient clinics. There, they would get important practical experience and on-the-spot, one-on-one teaching from their more experienced compatriots, from LARC doctors and nurses, and from me during non-class hours.

There was immediate agreement between Susan and I that we should use *Where There Is No Doctor* as the textbook. In fact, she had been working to accumulate a supply of the books for some time in advance of my arrival. I had brought several copies with me from the United States and several more were already on hand. The latter had been donated by GOAL, an Irish relief agency.

One of the first refugees to whom I was introduced at Wad Sherife was Josef, a young artist, who could paint the medical illustrations I would use as visual aids. Before my arrival, he already had turned out colorful anatomical diagrams of the lungs, digestive system and an ear on three-foot-square pieces of particleboard. Whenever I needed another illustration, I could lend Josef a book with a picture of what I wanted. He'd reproduce it, in full color, in a matter of days.

Susan suggested I spend the first week or so observing and evaluating the students. Many of them were already in the clinics receiving informal on-the-job training. This would help me decide what I needed to teach them. For two weeks, I spent alternate days with my future students at Wad Sherife and with my typewriter and books at the LARC house in Kassala. I consulted Susan almost daily, partly to seek her advice, party looking for reassurance as I wrote the course outline and began writing lesson plans.

We decided I would teach some basic anatomy and physiology, going through the body, system by system, part by part, from top to bottom. I would also teach how to recognize and treat the diseases and conditions that corresponded with each part of the body as we went along. And I would teach and have the students practice any pertinent procedures as we went along.

For example, I planned to talk early in the course about the anatomy and physiology of the eye and how to recognize and treat the eye diseases most commonly seen at Wad Sherife. Conjunctivitis and eye conditions caused by vitamin A deficiency were rampant. Then we would go from the classroom to a feeding center where, one by one, each student would identify a child with conjunctivitis. The student would clean the child's eyes, treat them with tetracycline eye ointment and teach the child's mother about continuing care and how to prevent spread of the infection to other children.

We decided that in every lesson I should emphasize the importance to the refugee health care workers of teaching preventative medicine and self-care to the masses. I planned to put special emphasis on the prevention, recognition and treatment of what statistically had been shown to be the most common health problems among the refugee population. These were eye and ear infections, colds, flu, pneumonia, tuberculosis, meningitis, anemia, malaria and the various diarrhea diseases—dysentery, giardia and cholera.

My confidence grew day by day as I built a curriculum around this basic plan. I wrote outlines of my daily lesson plans, although I hadn't the faintest idea how to translate a given amount of information typed on a sheet of paper into a framework of time spent teaching in a classroom. This was partly due to my lack of teaching experience and partly because I was uncertain how well the students would understand me. I couldn't even estimate how fast I would be able to go. Susan had even anticipated this potential problem. Part of her criteria for selecting these particular 12 men and one woman as the first group of students was their ability to speak English.

Time didn't really matter anyway, beyond the length of each daily class, which ran from about 7:30 to 10 a.m. I could teach until we thought I'd taught enough. It didn't matter if the class ended in August or November or February. We didn't have to get done in time for anybody to go on summer vacation. Nobody was going anywhere but me. When my time was up, someone else would replace me and continue the class, from wherever I had left off.

I had become impatient to get started as we approached June 10th, the day of the first class. I was tired of merely being an observer at Wad Sherife. I was also tired of staying behind in Kassala with my books and typewriter while everyone else on the LARC team was at the camp actively helping. I was starting to feel confident about my ability to teach subjects in which I was experienced. I even looked forward to the days when we'd talk about tropical diseases, when I expected to learn as much as I'd teach.

In fact, I had only one real worry as I went through the final days of preparation. I wondered if I would ever be able to remember the students' names. They looked like they'd been created at random from a can of alphabet soup.

Medhani Zerom.
Tesfomichel Bahta.
Zemuy Ghebreheskel.
Mehari Endrias.
Kubrom Humed.
Fuzum Tewelde.
Manna Gebru.

Hassan Idris.
Ghebrehewet Abraha.
Teclezim Ghebreweld.
Arafat Hazot.
Ghebrehiwet Habte.
Samuel Jamie. Hooray for Samuel!

EIGHT

If anyone had taken a survey of the refugees at Wad Sherife, asking them one by one where they had come from, only a handful of the 70,000 men, women and children would have said "Ethiopia." They would have been almost unanimous in saying they were from Eritrea. Only a few of us had even heard of Eritrea before arriving at Wad Sherife.

Eritrea at the time was a large province in Ethiopia, forming its entire Red Sea coastline from Sudan in the north to Djibouti in the south. According to most Eritreans, it wasn't part of Ethiopia at all. The Italians had colonized Eritrea in 1889. Over the next 50-plus years, they established farms, irrigation systems, factories, railways, roads and seaports. By the 1940s, Eritrea had reached such a state of industrialization that 20 percent of its population had given up their tribal ways and moved to the towns and cities, the largest of which is Asmara, the capital.

Eritreans from Asmara spoke fondly of their former home, calling it Little Rome. Indeed, photos they inevitably brought out showed a European-looking city with broad boulevards, divided down the center by well-tended gardens. The streets were mostly paved, they said, and the city was immaculately clean. Eritreans from the cities seemed to be culturally closer to Europeans than to other east Africans I met. This, no doubt, was because of their longtime ties with the Italians and because large numbers of them were Christians rather than Muslims, as were the majority of people in this part of Africa.

Many were highly educated as well. Among my students, Zemuy had been a teacher in Eritrea and spoke seven languages. Manna's husband Ghebru had been a judge and spoke English, French and a number of African languages. Josef, the artist, could write in three different scripts: Roman, with its 26 letters written from left to right; Arabic, with its 28 characters written from right to left; and his native Amharic, which had about 250 characters and was written left to right.

Eritrea remained an Italian colony until the British defeated the Italians there during World War II. The peace treaty at the end of the war stated that the fate of Italy's former colonies be decided by the United States, Britain, France and the Soviet Union. The British, who would maintain control of Eritrea until 1952, recommended partition of Eritrea between Ethiopia and Sudan, even though this was unacceptable to all of Eritrea's political parties. The United States was hardly less sensitive about the rights of self-determination and independence of the Eritreans. Said American Secretary of State John Foster Dulles: "From the point of view of justice, the opinions of the Eritrean people must receive consideration. Nevertheless, the strategic interest of the United States in the Red Sea basin and consideration of security and world peace make it necessary that the country has to be linked to our ally, Ethiopia."

A United Nations commission was sent to Eritrea to come up with an equitable plan. Not even the UN committee could agree on the question of independence versus union with Ethiopia. Finally, the UN General Assembly recommended Eritrea become an autonomous state with its own legislature, executive and judicial powers over domestic affairs but be under the federal sovereignty of Ethiopia.

Eritrea's autonomy remained intact, on paper, for approximately

10 years. In fact, the Ethiopian government of Emperor Haile Selassie, supported by the United States (which had replaced the British in Eritrea in 1953), began taking away the Eritreans' major rights almost immediately. First, Eritrean political parties were banned. Then Tigrinya, the official language of Eritrea, was suppressed and replaced by Amharic, the language of Ethiopia. Eritrean complaints to the United Nations about such blatant violations of the agreement were largely ignored.

Armed resistance against the Ethiopians began with the formation of the Eritrean Liberation Front (ELF) in 1961. The following year, Ethiopia dissolved the UN agreement and annexed Eritrea as one of its provinces. Guerilla activities increased. The EPLF (Eritrean People's Liberation Front), a splinter organization formed in 1970, fought along side the ELF to regain lost rights. As Eritrean resistance increased, so did reprisals by the Ethiopian government. Numerous arrests were made, detainees were tortured, factories were dismantled, and crops and villages were burned.

In 1974, Haile Selassie was overthrown. Amon Andom, head of Ethiopia's new military government, proposed a return to peace and the original UN agreement on Eritrean autonomy. However, Andom was assassinated three months later on orders from Menghistu Haile Mariam, who headed the Ethiopian government up into the eighties. Civil war between Eritrea and Ethiopia continued unabated throughout Mariam's rule. From 1977 on, Ethiopia drew strong support from the Soviet Union, which like the United States saw the strategic value of Eritrea's 500-mile Red Sea coastline.

There would be days at Wad Sherife, during July and August, when the reality of this 25-year-old war would appear alarmingly near. We could hear the bombing and gunfire from across the border.

Most of my students at Wad Sherife had gotten their first experience and training in health care by working as medics for the ELF or EPLF during the civil war. The Ethiopian government had drafted almost all of them, to fight alongside Cubans and Russians against the ELF and EPLF, they told me. All Eritrean men between the ages of 15 and 30 faced conscription into the Ethiopian army, they said, and were expected to help kill members of their own families in Eritrea. One of my students had become a widower while still in his early twenties. His wife of six months was killed by gunfire. Another had spent a year in solitary confinement in a military prison before he tricked a guard into letting him escape.

The Ethiopians also used the famine as a weapon in the civil war, refusing to distribute food to parts of Eritrea controlled by the ELF and EPLF. Of course, no government willingly feeds its enemy during time of war. With this background, it was easy to understand why the refugees considered themselves Eritreans rather than Ethiopians.

NINE

Sometimes, performing even the most mundane tasks could be incredibly difficult in Sudan. That's because much of the time, you just didn't feel well enough to want to do anything. You never quite knew when you'd feel well and when you wouldn't. One day you'd feel pretty well, the next day a little better, within an hour not so well, the next hour so-so.

Early on, I had a day when I didn't feel well at all. I didn't exactly feel bad, but in no way did I feel good. I felt totally and absolutely not good, as opposed to unwell or out and out bad. The feeling was so non-specific it defies description. It was unlike any feeling I'd ever had before.

It was a sizzling hot day and I was still working on my lesson plans prior to the beginning of classes. I had diarrhea and must have gone to squat in the latrine at the back of the garden a dozen times. Although we kept it as clean as possible, the latrine was a disgusting place. It was a little cubicle of a room with a round hole in the middle of a concrete floor. Actual toilets were unheard of in this part of the world. What made the latrine so revolting was that the hole in the floor was invariably ringed by hundreds of maggots. It wasn't any place to linger and read a magazine.

The latrine had actually prompted a lively discussion one morning about whether maggots shit, or whether they just ate shit, and if they did, who ate their shit. The question was never answered, but it was decided that if there was such a thing as maggot shit, it must be the lowest thing on earth.

Anyway, the feeling by which I was totally consumed on this particular day was one of overwhelming negative momentum. I was unable to halt my momentum, except I wasn't doing anything to halt in the first place.

I was forcing myself to do a little work on my lesson plans, but brief sittings at the typewriter were interspersed with long rests on my inside bed. We had inside beds and outside beds so we didn't have to drag them back and forth day and night. It would have been unthinkable to lie down outdoors during the day, but it was marginally cooler there at night. Most of us slept outside, at the end of the garden farthest from the latrine.

I made a futile attempt to keep cool by posturing myself so the least possible area of my body came in contact with the bed. I lay flat on my back, feet apart and knees apart to form a tripod between my feet and my butt. My arms were extended over my head and my hands held onto the frame at the head of the bed. I lay perfectly still. I wanted the absolute maximum exposure to circulating air. I wanted to expend the least possible amount of energy. The only thing able to break the inertia was the recurrent urge to go to the latrine. Once moved that far, I could return to my typewriter, until I again felt compelled to lie down.

Even a shower was not an appealing idea. The shower was a good 20 yards away at the other end of the house and I didn't want to walk that far. Plus, the water came out so hot during the middle of the day that you had to let it run for several minutes before you dared get under it. Still, the fact that we had running water in Kassala was a great morale builder.

All eight of us in the house took two or three cold showers day. We'd take one before leaving for camp at 7:00 in the morning, another after returning around 3:30 in the afternoon, and another immediately before going to bed, around 9:00 o'clock. The only way to be assured of being cool enough to fall asleep was to take that last cold shower just before going to bed. Like most of the others, I slept out in the open air at night, wearing only my shorts, without any covers.

Everyone had the kind of days I was having. No one felt really well every day and no one expected to. You just hoped you wouldn't have too many really bad days. Kassala was terribly dirty compared to North American or European cities and our immune systems needed time to adjust. You had to be infected by an organism before you could develop immunity to it. If you picked a number at random, say 25, and postulated that there were 25 viruses in Sudan that you'd never been exposed to at home, then you could expect to get 25 different infections from your first 25 encounters with these organisms. Fortunately, most were low-grade sub-clinical infections. That means they didn't do much more than leave you feeling somewhere between not too well and pretty awful, but not for long. As the Sudanese were so fond of saying, *malesh*, never mind, what can you do?

Vic wondered aloud one day if anyone had ever done a study on the immune system of goats, which thrived in Kassala. We never saw any sick goats lying around. Goats had the city garbage disposal franchise. You dumped your garbage in the dirt street in front of your house. Next time you looked it was gone, having been eaten by the herd of goats that lingered at almost every street corner. If anything were biodegradable, a goat would eat it. This was part of a marvelous ecological cycle. The goats cleaned the streets and turned the garbage into milk for their owners. Unfortunately for the goats, a few of them got barbecued every time there was a special feast day.

Good health was no guarantee that one would have limitless energy. In such intense heat, it was necessary to have a time-energy framework in which to function. If you stepped outside the boundaries, you paid. If you stayed up too late one night, you paid the next day. Stay out in the direct sun too long, you pay. Try to accomplish an unreasonable amount of work, pay. It took each of us a time to recognize our own limits, to accept that our capacities for any kind of physical activity were only a fraction of what they had been at home. For a group as highly motivated as ours, this was extremely frustrating

I remember staying up until 11:00 o'clock one night after we drove to Girba for a surprise birthday party for Karen Kruger, an American pediatrician working at another LARC refugee camp. I willed myself to put in my six or seven hours work at camp the next day. Once home that afternoon, I collapsed in a semi-paralytic state into a chair in the back garden. I was unable to move again for more than three hours, unable to get out of the chair.

As soon as we had gotten home from Wad Sherife, I made a tomato and cheese sandwich, got a glass of water and settled down to rest for what I thought would be a few minutes. Then I read the entire section on Sudan from a travel guide to Africa, writing down as I went along several words that I wanted to remember how to spell. I wrote them in ink on the palm of my left hand because I didn't have the energy to get up and find a piece of paper. Then I ate dinner without moving from the chair. I stayed there while someone else cleared the table, had a cup of coffee, and spent another hour talking with Bob Enik about the Beatles, Liverpool and London.

Eventually, I got up to go to the latrine. Then, having escaped the chair trap, I kept my momentum going and moved on to the shower. There, before I realized it, I washed my hand of all the words I'd copied from the guidebook. *Malesh*. Never mind, what can you do.

TEN

We welcomed the cholera outbreak to Wad Sherife with the same enthusiasm that medieval Europe must have had for the plague. We had three cases one day. Six more the next. Then 12. Then 30. If the number continued to rise exponentially for more than another few days, we would be seeing hundreds and then shortly, God forbid, thousands of new cases a day. There was no way in the world we could have stemmed the tide then. An epidemic of such magnitude would have meant certain death for thousands or even tens of thousands of human beings.

Our reaction to the possible catastrophe was swift and we hoped it would be on target. This was neither the time nor place for errors in judgment.

As soon as the first case had been identified, the Swiss Red Cross turned one of the children's wards in its hospital into a cholera isolation ward. We built a five-bed ward the same afternoon, safely away from the rest of the patients in our inpatient clinic. Susan Smith and the Swiss medical director had decided within hours of the first case being found that we needed to combine forces to head off impending disaster, which could sweep through all sections of the camp, theirs as well as ours, without discrimination.

By the second day we were transferring each new case we diagnosed to the Swiss Red Cross cholera ward, sending patients across camp in a *boxie* hired to be used as an ambulance. A *boxie* is the cheapest form of short distance public transport in eastern Sudan. It is generally a small Toyota pickup truck with end-to-end padded bench seats in the back and a roof to shield riders from the sun. The sides are open to the air and entry is from the rear. Cholera is so contagious that one *boxie* had to be reserved for cholera patients, their families and health care workers only. The driver had to take prophylactic treatment against cholera. He also had to disinfect his *boxie* every night.

Construction of a large cholera isolation hospital began within days on an isolated piece of ground midway between the SRC and LARC hospitals. Two army tents, each capable of holding 25 beds, went up first. They were followed in rapid succession by a large rectangular structure built with poles and mats, with room for about 70 beds. There was a convalescent building of similar construction, with mats covering the ground, rather than beds, for those requiring only oral rehydration and oral antibiotic treatment. There was a reception area where possible admissions could be held until positively diagnosed. One of the tents was used to store food, cases of intravenous fluids and other supplies. A cooking area was built with separate washing-up facilities for contaminated cups and bowls, and for clean ones. A water tank was brought in and latrines and waste disposal pits were dug. And finally, a six-feet-high fence was built around the complex to keep uninfected people from wandering in and infected ones from leaving before they had completed their treatment.

Within a week, Eritrean health care workers from both SRC and LARC were working around the clock to staff the hospital. SRC and LARC expatriates worked together as supervisors during the day and worked the night shift on alternate nights—SRC one night, LARC the next.

The first case of cholera was diagnosed as I was finalizing the outline for my course, hours before classes were to begin. I had planned to teach the lessons in a deliberate sequence, beginning with some important basics. I planned a continuity of subjects from day to day. Instead, we now would begin by learning about cholera and two closely related subjects, dehydration and rehydration; and three skills needed in assessing and treating cholera patients, blood pressure reading, pulse assessment and inserting IVs.

I taught my first class about cholera less than three days after seeing my first case of it. Before the week was out, my students were standing up in front of groups in feeding centers, clinics and outpatient waiting areas—anywhere large groups of people could be found—as teachers themselves. They taught their fellow refugees about prevention and recognition of cholera, the urgency of seeking immediate treatment once infected, and the importance of prophylactic treatment for all family members of anyone who had become infected.

Even the Sudanese became involved, although the government categorically denied there was any cholera in Sudan. The army set up several checkpoints on the route from Wad Sherife to Kassala, to assure no one except health care workers and those delivering supplies passed between the city and camp. They didn't want anyone bringing the dreaded "gastroenteritis," as they called it, from the refugee camp to the city.

The checkpoints were a joke. One might have called them roadblocks, had there been any roads. We traveled back and forth across the desert between home and camp each day using landmarks as guideposts. A few of the landmarks were trees, a tree being a very lonesome figure and prominent landmark in this part of Sudan. Beneath each tree would be three or four teenaged soldiers in green khaki fatigues, holding ancient M-1 rifles, and looking very much like they'd rather be somewhere cooler than out in the middle of the desert. I thought of them as Sudanese sundials. You could almost tell the time of day by observing which side of the tree they were sitting on, seeking the maximum amount of shade.

The most laughable thing about the checkpoints was that they were so easily avoided, if one was determined to do so. The trees and soldiers were few and far between and there were no roads to restrict where one drove. You could drive around the checkpoints undetected, or at least without being stopped, simply by driving a circuitous route away from the trees. It's doubtful the soldiers had orders to shoot and they had no vehicles with which to chase illegal passers-by. A number of people must have done exactly that, for cholera spread to some of the villages on the very fringe of Kassala. We heard reports of people dying there without having been treated.

The immediate implementation of our plan at Wad Sherife was a success, in the short term at least. We had few deaths and most of those were attributable to the fact that the victims hadn't come in for treatment soon enough. The number of cases leveled off at approximately 30 per day. While this caused a great deal of stress for both Eritrean and *khawaja* staff and to our limited supplies, it was neither unbearable nor unmanageable. If the admission rate would stay at 30 per day, we would somehow manage.

ELEVEN

Mary Bowe was a nurse and ambulance driver from County Tipperary, one of a large number of Irish volunteers I met wherever I went in Sudan. She had been sent to work with the LARC team at Wad Sherife by GOAL, an Irish relief agency that paid the expenses to send Irish medical people to Africa to work with other relief organizations that had a particular need to fill. For example, a nurse was assigned here, a midwife there, a doctor somewhere else.

There were two GOAL nurses on the LARC team, Phena Cullen and Mary. The medical director and one of the physicians on the Swiss Red Cross team, Joe Carragher, was Irish. Lalmba Association had a GOAL midwife, Mary O'Brien, at its camp in Wad el Hilewu. GOAL's work in Sudan was coordinated by an energetic, strikingly attractive, blond-haired Irish woman, Ann Bourke, who also spent time running an immunization program in Kenya. I met other GOAL people whose names I've forgotten and heard of others working in the west of Sudan with refugees from the famine in Chad. GOAL also provided many of the textbooks for my classes at Wad Sherife and at three other camps where I would teach later.

The good will of the Irish didn't stop there. Live Aid, the hugely successful fund raising project, was both inspired and orchestrated by Irish rock musician Bob Geldof. It was seen on television around the world by an estimated 1.5 billion people and resulted in $70 million in donations. The people of Ireland gave more money per capita than any other nation. It was impossible not to be touched by the social conscience of this small island nation, with a population of less than 3.5 million.

While American physician Vic Snyder provided us with our daily ration of *M*A*S*H** style humor, Mary Bowe occasionally put on a show comparable to the best of *Animal House*. Nobody was immune to her sudden urges to throw cups, glasses or even buckets of water when they were least expected. If it was mealtime and she didn't have mayonnaise smeared across her chin, you half wondered if it was really Mary sitting across the table from you, or an imposter. Once, she took a large bowl containing a partially eaten dessert made of jello, jam and fruit, and turned it upside down over her head. She'd do anything for a laugh.

Mary was also a spectacular dancer and an extremely athletic person. When she danced, her feet appeared only rarely to touch the floor. She never passed up an opportunity to kick up her heels. It was not unusual to find her singing, clapping and dancing for the children at the feeding center where she worked. In the beginning, the Eritrean children didn't quite know what to make of her. Eventually, they were swept up by her spirit and enthusiasm, and clapped and sang along with her. The stimulation was good for the children. They always seemed to eat better on days when there was entertainment or activity for them. It was a sad day for them when Mary left the feeding center to work fulltime in the cholera isolation hospital.

At home in Ireland, Mary had once won the County Tipperary women's golf championship. And on this particular June morning in Kassala, she had gotten up at 5:15 to go for a run along the River Gash with Vic, Bob Enik and me.

I was staying at home in Kassala that day to finalize my course outline and lesson plans. It was a Friday and classes would begin Monday. At 7:00 o'clock, following breakfast, Mary left with the others to go to Wad Sherife. I didn't expect to see her again until at least 3:00 in the afternoon.

At 11:30, there was a knock on our front gate. I went to answer. When I opened the green corrugated metal gate, I was stunned to see Mary, white as a Sudanese *jallabia.* She was so sick she barely had the strength to stand without support. She had been struck by a sudden and debilitating attack of diarrhea and vomiting at camp. Johannes, our Eritrean handyman and driver, had driven her back to Kassala so I could look after her at the house. Six hours earlier, we had been running together along the river. Now, she looked about three-quarters dead.

I sent Johannes back to Wad Sherife with a note asking the others to bring a supply of oral rehydration solution and tetracycline capsules when they came home in the afternoon. I didn't know if Mary had cholera. I still hadn't seen a case firsthand. She had the symptoms, though, and I could see she was already badly dehydrated.

As soon as Johannes had gone, I regretted not having asked for intravenous fluids, tubing and a needle with which to connect an IV to one of Mary's veins. Once he had gone, there was no way I could make contact with Wad Sherife. There were no telephones, I had no vehicle, and it was unthinkable to try walking that far in the heat of day. Anyway, I couldn't leave Mary alone.

I made a bed for Mary in the unused room at the far end of the house and got her two buckets, one to vomit in and the other to use as a toilet. She was too weak to walk to the latrine. I then concocted a rehydration drink as best I could. We had salt and sugar in our kitchen, but no potassium or bicarbonate of soda. All four are needed to fully replace body electrolytes lost through prolonged diarrhea and vomiting.

I helped Mary walk to the shower to try to cool her down. This was a somewhat futile exercise since the water came out of the tap hot in the middle of the day. Mary was so unsteady on her feet that I feared she might pass out in the shower before the water ran long enough to cool down. I didn't want to have to drag her the length of the garden to get her back to bed. I decided the safest way to keep her cool was to point two electric fans at her and splash water over her periodically.

Mary was so weak and her color so pale that I genuinely worried about what would happen if she deteriorated further. The first time I offered her a jar of rehydration fluid, she dropped in on the bed. She dropped another on the floor. She was having a hard time staying awake. She didn't want to drink because she kept vomiting. The only thing that made her move voluntarily was the urge to sit on the bucket. Her stools looked like cloudy water, a classic sign of cholera. I wished the others would hurry and get back from Wad Sherife. I felt terribly alone and inadequate for not having requested supplies to administer intravenous fluids.

Then, almost as suddenly as she had gotten so violently ill, Mary began to recover. The diarrhea stopped two hours after Johannes had delivered her to the gate. She began to drink, quite willingly. By the next morning her cheeks were pink again. And by dinnertime the next day, she looked like the Mary we were used to seeing at the table every evening. She had a smear of mayonnaise across one of her cheeks.

TWELVE

Few others in our group ever became as sick as Mary, but we all suffered from varying degrees of malnutrition and weight loss due to constant diarrhea. We had plenty to eat in Kassala, but it often went in one end and out the other before our bodies had time to absorb any nutrients. Once, Vic wrote a letter home, warning: "I won't take up as much room when I get back."

Karen Kruger, an American pediatrician at the LARC camp in Girba, was one *khawaja* who did get sicker than Mary. She contracted hepatitis. A tiny person to begin with, her weight dropped way below 100 pounds before she recovered.

When I got home to California in November, I weighed 109 pounds. I had avoided serious illness, except for a brief bout with malaria, but there were extenuating circumstances. I spent more than two months at a Lalmba camp in Wad el Hileu, quite accurately described by someone once as "as far away as you'll ever want to get from anywhere."

From there, a city of 100,000 such as Kassala seemed to represent planet earth itself. We had no electricity, no running water, not much food, and were six hours from the nearest post office. With no electricity, we had no refrigeration and therefore no cold drinking water and no capability for storing perishable foods.

I remember eating a mustard sandwich for lunch one day, with crackers and date jam for dessert, crackers and mustard after that because the aftertaste was better, and four glasses of tepid water. One night for dinner, four of us shared five tomatoes, one cucumber, a pot of boiled noodles and cups of hot chocolate made from cocoa, sugar, powdered milk and water. Someone said the hot chocolate tasted "like a candy bar left floating in the bathtub overnight."

We had no reason to feel sorry for ourselves in Kassala. Fresh fruit and vegetables were plentiful in the *souk*, or open-air market, seven days a week. Hundreds of vendors squatted on mats on the ground, all day long beneath the blazing sun, selling tomatoes, onions, grapefruit, limes and bananas. Occasionally there were cucumbers, eggplant, pumpkins or okra. Sometimes there were a few golf ball-sized potatoes. Once in a while there were sweet potatoes. One time, I saw two bunches of finger-sized carrots. I bought them both.

There were guavas when it was guava season, mangoes during the all-too-short mango season and something purported to be an orange. This fruit was green on the outside, pale yellow on the inside and contained a flavorless juice. Its texture inside and out left little doubt that it was a citrus fruit. It was some sort of a generic citric fruit.

Once in a very great while there were watermelons. I don't think I ever tasted anything better than an ice-cold watermelon on a 115-degree afternoon.

We also could get the ingredients to make peanut butter sandwiches in the *souk*. Excellent unleavened bread, made from coarsely ground grain, was baked morning and evening in primitive-looking beehive ovens, fueled with charcoal. It was sold hot as it came out of the ovens for only a few piasters. Freshly ground peanut butter was sold by half a dozen women, squatting on the ground in a group, near the meat market. They kept their peanut butter in brightly colored enamel bowls and sold it by the estimated weight. You were expected to bring your own container, maybe an old jar or even a plastic bag. If you didn't have one, they wrapped the peanut butter in a piece of newspaper. I've never tasted better bread or peanut butter anywhere.

The meat market might best be described as the meat and fly market. Meat and flies go together in a Third World market like meat and potatoes in some other parts of the world. They're meant for each other. Meat and potatoes, meat and flies.

Animals in Muslim countries are slaughtered and butchered daily, so meat is always fresh. Good thing, because there was no refrigeration in the *souk*. Every part of the animals was for sale. Body parts hung from hooks and were laid out on concrete slabs. There were intestines covered with flies. Livers covered with flies. Camels' heads covered with flies. Sometimes, there were so many flies you could barely see the meat.

Worse than a camel's head or the hind leg of a goat black with flies, though, was a piece of red meat that didn't have flies on it. It didn't take us long to figure out, after seeing this oddity a few times, that it probably had been sprayed with an insecticide. Even worse, it probably was DDT since that was the cheapest and most commonly used insecticide in Sudan. Meat was not a big part of our diet after we came to that conclusion.

Another fresh food we avoided was chicken. We bought a live chicken once, partially out of sympathy as I recall. It was barely alive and looked to be a victim of severe malnutrition and dehydration. We kept it for a few days, feeding and watering it in the hope of fattening it up. Then, some of the people in the house turned sentimental and didn't want to kill it. They most definitely didn't want to eat it. In the end, the majority prevailed and the chicken was put to death, but there was no part worth eating. There was nothing beneath the feathers except skin and bones.

The best way to eat a chicken in Kassala was before it came out of its egg. Eggs were available most days, sold individually or in neat little piles of five, by a few women who squatted on the ground near the peanut butter ladies.

While fresh food was available for next to nothing in the *souk*, one could spend a small fortune, relatively speaking, buying imported packaged foods from such grocery shops as Kassala House, Yemen House and London House. A box of Egyptian cornflakes, as much a staple at our breakfast table as the BBC world news on Vic's short wave radio, cost about $3.00. That was a bargain, considering you could eat the cornflakes and the cardboard box, if you liked, with little noticeable change in flavor.

We ate our cornflakes with reconstituted powdered milk six mornings a week. On the seventh, we bought fresh raw milk from a milkman who came through our neighborhood, selling door to door, from two large cans that hung from the sides of his donkey. The best that could be said of the powdered milk was that it was a good match for the instant coffee.

We ate lunch when we returned from camp at about 3:30 each afternoon. Lunch was less repetitious than breakfast. Sometimes we ate tomato sandwiches, sometimes cheese sandwiches made from Kraft canned processed cheese, and sometimes tomato and cheese sandwiches. For variety, we had peanut butter sandwiches, banana sandwiches or peanut butter and banana sandwiches.

We also ate two other meals each day. Refugee cooks prepared a 10:00 o'clock breakfast for all workers at Wad Sherife, Eritrean and *khawaja* alike. Everyone got a large plastic cup of hot sweet tea, a piece of bread and a bowl of hot food. The hot food might be plain noodles, onions cooked in oil, noodles and onions mixed, beans and onions, or lentils. This became so monotonous that even the refugees sometimes complained.

Our dinner each night was prepared by a 14-year-old Eritrean girl, Ailynn, who we employed to cook, clean house and wash our clothes. She worked for us six days a week. We paid about $45 a month for her services. She made a salad every day of bananas and grapefruit, with only one variation; mangoes were added to the mix when they were in season. The remainder of the meal was prepared from lentils, rice, noodles or spaghetti, and combinations of whatever vegetables were available that day.

The choice of vegetables was closely related to the whims of Gibrab, a young Eritrean who did our shopping for us. He brought the food back to Ailynn in a basket on the back of his bicycle. For a long time, he didn't necessarily bring back anything on the shopping list we gave him each morning. That was predictable since we wrote the list in English, which was his third-most proficient language, after Tigrinya and Arabic. We tried to clarify the shopping list with pictures but gave that up after someone drew a picture of okra and he brought back sweet potatoes.

We got better results after I went to the *souk* with Gibrab one morning. Together, we identified every different fruit and vegetable we could find and wrote out a bilingual list.

Like everyone else, Gibrab had a day off every week, plus holidays, so we had to do our own shopping at least once a week. Whoever happened to be home in Kassala on Gibrab's day off did the shopping for that night's dinner. This was not always accomplished without difficulty. The first time I went shopping, I didn't know how much to pay for anything. There were no established or posted prices.

I knew how to ask "how much?" and I could count to 10 in Arabic. However, I seldom could understand when spoken to, especially if someone said something like "1.25 for this little pile of onions here." It was also possible to ask how much something cost and be told five pounds, then make a counter offer of two pounds and eventually settle on three pounds. Gibrab might have paid only one pound.

After a short time, I figured out a way to determine a reasonable price. I stood next to someone buying the same thing I wanted and watched to see how much he or she paid. I then bought the same thing from the same vendor and handed over the same amount of money without discussion. This worked well. One day I bought four grapefruit, three mangoes, two bunches of carrots, half a kilo (1.1 pounds) of okra, 1.5 kilos of bananas, a cucumber, a watermelon, six eggs and a hand-woven shopping basket for 11 pounds 65 piasters, about $3.50.

I used the same tactics in the meat market. I watched a woman pay for a fresh slab of flesh, which the butcher dropped, unwrapped, directly onto her fruit and vegetables in her shopping bag. After paying five piasters to a small boy for a plastic bag to catch and carry the meat in, I ordered the same. I never found out whether I'd bought beef, lamb or camel.

By the time I'd bought peanut butter in addition to the fruit, vegetables and meat, I had passed more than two hours in the *souk* but had spent less than $6.00. That was the price of a single jar of Tang in one of the shops that sold imported processed foods.

THIRTEEN

Sometimes it seemed like all the flies in the world had descended on Kassala at once. One generation invaded our latrine and laid its eggs there. The next was born and raised there. On days when the fly count was particularly high, you had to look cross-eyed at your food before you took each bite, so you didn't eat the flies that were sharing your lunch. On those days, we held our sandwiches in one hand and waved the flies off with the other, immediately before taking each bite.

Flies had complete control over when we could sleep and when we could not. They vanished at about sunset each evening but reappeared next morning at the crack of dawn, walking across exposed parts of our bodies, tickling us out of our sleep. I tried to take an afternoon nap once but the flies wouldn't let me.

No matter how hard I tried, I couldn't outsmart them and find a way to fall asleep. It was the ultimate experience in frustration. My full-sized American human being brain could not outsmart a score or two of flies that had been raised from the time they were squirming white maggots on a diet of nothing but shit from the latrine in the back of our garden. How big is a fly's brain, anyway? I felt humiliated.

What did they want with me? I had just taken a shower so there wasn't anything to eat on me. I had dried off by squatting naked in front of a fan so there wasn't anything to drink. It should have been obvious I wasn't going anywhere, lying on a bed, so they weren't getting a ride anywhere.

Vic, Bob and I had decided during our run that very morning that flies do hop on people just for the ride. We had attempted to do a fly count on one another's backs as we ran along the bank of the River Gash at sunrise. Even though I am shorter and my shoulders less broad than either Bob's or Vic's, I had more flies on my back than either of them. The count was somewhere around 36, although a totally accurate count was impossible because there was always one more fly getting on or off.

Anyway, this was one of those hot afternoons when I didn't want to cover myself with a sheet to take a nap. When it's so hot, you don't want your body to touch any more of the bed or bedding than is absolutely necessary. You don't want any one part of your skin to touch another part of your skin. You wish you could suspend yourself in air.

The flies loved my dilemma. Any part of my body left exposed, they'd land on. Marybeth MaCarthy, who was also home on a day off, thought if we turned a fan directly onto me, we could blow the flies away. The combined knowledge accumulated in the brains of two adult human beings, totaling nearly three-quarters of a century, should have been enough to outsmart the smartest fly on earth. It wasn't.

The fan wasn't big enough to blow the files off the entire length of my body. They all descended on my ankles and neck, only now in greater concentration at these two wind-free axes. We adjusted the fan so it blew across me from the top of my head to my knees. I covered my lower legs with a sheet. This was a compromise on my part, an admission of at least partial defeat, but it gave me the upper hand. I think the flies went off for a conference somewhere. I dropped off to sleep for a few minutes.

Then they attacked again from the leeward side. The lee side of a thin man lying flat on his back with a fan blowing air across his body from right to left is not a very large area of sheltered skin surface. But then, how large a landing strip does a fly need? The left side of my body can accommodate more flies at once than most people would care to host in a lifetime.

Finally, I decided to use mind power. I told myself that flies didn't really bother me, that I couldn't feel them. Why should I feel a few flies? Flies aren't heavy. Flies don't have claws on their feet. Flies don't bite you. At that precise moment in my thought process, a fly walked up under my glasses and across my eyelid. I decided I really didn't want to take a nap after all.

FOURTEEN

The cholera outbreak continued unabated. We decided a Swiss Red Cross or LARC expatriate medical worker needed to be present at the isolation hospital at all times because many of the new cases were critically ill. Besides, new admissions were arriving in an unpredictable pattern. We feared that 20, 30 or more seriously ill people might all arrive within a period of a few hours. The Eritreans, working without our supervision, would be unable to cope.

Each of us had to take our turn working the night shift, which meant we had to be at the cholera hospital before dark and remain there until relieved at about 7:30 the next morning. Usually, the person on night duty worked all day at his or her regular job, went back to Kassala for a shower and dinner, returned to Wad Sherife to work all night, and then tried to sleep the next day.

Dr. Vic Snyder, who didn't like to take any time off, had his own personal schedule when it came his time to work the night shift. He worked all day, all night, all day again, and then caught up on his sleep. He caught up by taking a nap as soon as we got home from camp in the afternoon and going to bed again immediately after dinner. Once, Vic worked 35 days in a row with a couple of night shifts thrown in for good measure.

We were free to choose our own days off. We were supposed to take at least one a week, two if we liked. We had the option of saving up the second days off of each week until the end of the month and then taking up to five consecutive days off. No on ever took all his allotted time off.

I looked upon my first night at the cholera hospital as something of an adventure, in no small part because I had to drive myself from Kassala to Wad Sherife. I hadn't driven during my first month in Sudan and had no particular desire to do so. I hadn't thought to bring my driver's license from California, so I could have been put in jail if I'd been in an accident. As curious a person as I am, I had no desire to see the inside of a Sudanese jail.

I set out from Kassala at 6:00 o'clock in the evening in one of the Toyota four-wheel drive vehicles, hoping I would be able to find the cholera hospital. Usually a positive thinker, I was overwhelmed with negative thoughts. Would I remember all the landmarks in the desert, such as the gruesome-looking dried carcass of a camel, to guide me in the right direction? Had I left early enough to get there before dark? What if I got a flat tire? We had been averaging two or three a week. If I stopped to change a tire, it surely would get dark and I could be assured of getting lost. Would I even be able to change a tire? Once, Vic and I had tried to change a tire in the dark and couldn't figure out how to jack the vehicle high enough to get the flat tire clear of the ground. We had to dig a hole under the tire to get if off.

This particular Toyota was a jeep-style vehicle and the most uncomfortable thing, animal or mechanical, I had ever ridden. No one would ever buy a vehicle like this, I thought, if he took it on a test drive over rough terrain. I went over bumps on the way to Wad Sherife that literally catapulted me out of the driver's seat, leaving no part of me in contact with the vehicle except my hands on the steering wheel.

It was nearly dark when I found the cholera hospital. None of the flat-roofed pole-and-mat buildings was much over six or seven feet tall. They blended in with the flat horizon, even in broad daylight. There were no lights since there was no electricity. There were no road signs directing me to Wad Sherife since there were no roads. If I had left Kassala five minutes later, I wouldn't have been able to find the hospital, nor would I have been able to find my way back home.

During the half-hour drive across the desert, I also worried whether I'd be able to handle the medical problems. As a nurse in British and American hospitals, I was accustomed to picking up a phone and calling a doctor to solve life and death problems. Tonight I would need to make urgent treatment decisions on my own. I would be totally in command, making all decisions for the cholera unit for the next 13 hours. I would diagnose new patients, order their treatments and perform the most difficult procedures. I had three Eritrean medical assistants to work with, each very good in his own right, but worlds apart from me in training and experience. I had good help but no one to lean on.

We started the night with 25 or 30 patients. Almost every one had IV fluids infusing into his or her arm. Most were vomiting or suffering from severe diarrhea, or both. They were all very sick. Furthermore, everyone looked extra black in the dark of night. We had no lights in the hospital except a few gas lanterns and some flashlights whose batteries were nearer to death than many of the patients.

Because some of the patients were so severely dehydrated, we ran intravenous fluids into them as fast as they would go. Some were infused at a steady stream instead of drop by drop, a dangerous procedure unless you can closely monitor the patient's reaction to it. This was necessary during the first half-hour or so to treat severe dehydration, accompanied by protracted diarrhea and vomiting. In addition to monitoring the patients' tolerance to their IV therapy, we had to make sure the containers of fluid didn't run dry and veins didn't break down, allowing fluid to run into the surrounding tissue of their arms.

As soon as I arrived, I made a walking round of all the patients with my Eritrean assistants. We assessed each patient and talked about what we would be doing with him or her during the night. This took more than two hours, as we had to assess the rate and amplitude of the pulse of each patient, measure blood pressures and use stethoscopes to listen to the lungs of several others. We had to hang several new bags of IV fluids and coax people to drink oral rehydration solution. We also had to question each patient about whether he was still having diarrhea and vomiting, and ask if he was passing any urine.

In severe dehydration, urine output stops. Conversely, the resumption of urination indicates a person is becoming hydrated and IV infusions can be slowed down or stopped, depending on whether the person is able to take oral fluids.

Checking the amount and consistency of a person's diarrhea and vomiting was a simple matter of looking in the buckets. One was placed beside the head of every bed for vomit and another directly under each bed for diarrhea. Diarrhea is so protracted and debilitating that many cholera patients are unable to get out of bed to pass a stool. They must be cared for on special beds that have a hole in the middle. The diarrhea stools pass through the hole in the bed into the bucket.

After finishing our rounds at about 9:00 o'clock, I stumbled through the dark to the cooking area at the other side of the compound, where I sat down to have a cup of tea and bowl of rice. I had taken a few sips of tea but hadn't even tasted the rice when someone ran across from the reception area to tell me there was a new patient I needed to see immediately. So much for tea and rice.

The new arrival was a little girl, about five years old, who was very close to death. I could feel no pulses in her wrists or feet. I thought for a moment she might already be dead, but I accidentally hit her head with my flashlight and she responded by turning away. We carried her across the compound as quickly as we could and laid her on a bed. One of the Eritreans made a tourniquet by holding her arm tightly in the hope we could find a vein into which to put an IV needle. Another obtained the child's history from her father, who had brought her in on a donkey. My responsibility was to insert a hollow needle into a vein so we could hydrate her, but she was so dehydrated there were no veins to be seen. They had all collapsed owing to the

71

low volume of fluid in her body. They must have been tiny to start with in such a small child anyway. She was very black and the only light we could shine directly onto her arms was from a dim flashlight. Her chances seemed bleak. I knew she could die momentarily, even if I did manage to get a needle in. We might not be able to put enough fluids in during the first half hour to resuscitate her.

Unfortunately, it didn't occur to me to pass a tube through her nose to her stomach, as is sometimes done with unconscious patients. We could have begun hydrating her through this tube while searching for a suitable vein through which to give IV fluids.

I cleansed her upper arm with a disinfectant where I thought I felt a tiny vein. I pushed a tiny needle through her skin—and into the vein. I don't ever recall working under such pressure. I was aware the whole time that her life was entirely in my hands, and that I was in God's. I prayed as I worked.

I had found such a tiny vein and inserted such a tiny needle that the fluids would run in only very slowly. She was not out of the woods yet. She still could die any minute. After about five minutes, the vein ruptured spontaneously. We were back where we started. We had to find another vein into which to put another needle. I searched for 10 minutes, in deep concentration, but this time could neither see nor feel one. Time was running out.

Then one of the Eritreans with a sensitive fingertip felt a vein on the child's other arm. Again, I got a needle in. This one stayed, with the aid of an arm splint we made from a piece of cardboard torn off a carton of intravenous fluids from Finland. After about half a liter of fluid had gone into the little girl, her veins began to fill and one of the Eritreans managed to put a larger needle into another vein. We were then able to hydrate her through two needles at once.

I was quick to point out to the Eritreans that we now had to be careful not to over hydrate this child, as we could easily cause her lungs to fill with fluid and her heart to fail. I went for my tea and rice, satisfied they understood.

I had not seen anyone before as dehydrated as this little girl when her father brought her in. I don't recall how long she had been having diarrhea and vomiting before she arrived. Nothing mattered during those first minutes except getting the IV started because that was all that could save her. I reflected that this was what disaster relief medical care was all about, improvisational treatment all the way. Donkey ambulances, dim flashlights, splints torn from discarded cardboard boxes.

By the time I finished my tea and rice, 10:00 o'clock and come and gone. Three others, who would work the rest of the night with me, had relieved my Eritrean assistants. All of us would be relieved at 7:30 next morning. I did another round of the patients with the new group of medical assistants and then began to think about lying down to get some sleep.

There was a crudely built shelter in one of the far corners of the compound where night staff could rest. It was equipped only with two wood frame beds with ropes stretched tightly, back and forth between the sides and ends of the frames. The beds looked like primitive pieces of garden furniture. There were no pillows, no mattresses, no palm mats to lie across the ropes. I was not bothered by the impending discomfort. I was so tired I thought I could drop off to sleep, if only temporarily, even if I had to stand on my head in the corner.

I had mixed feelings about trying to sleep, though. I left instructions with the Eritreans to wake me immediately if they had any problems, and I fully expected they would. Joe Carragher, the Swiss Red Cross doctor who had worked the night before, had been up most of the night because there had been eight new admissions.

I was more fortunate than Joe. There were no further admissions during the night. Nobody woke me. I slept from midnight until 5:00 o'clock. Best of all, when I made my morning rounds of the patients, the first I saw was the little girl we had admitted almost dead the night before. She was sitting on the side of a bed with her father, drinking oral rehydration solution from an orange plastic cup.

FIFTEEN

Even if we had the energy after working all day at Wad Sherife, there was little to do during our time off in the evening. I read in a guidebook that the Sudanese considered Kassala the Paris of eastern Sudan. It is true, there really was nothing to compare to it within a day's bus ride in any direction. But Paris?

I liked Kassala. It looked like an African city looked in my mind's eye before I ever saw one. Almost all the low, flat-roofed buildings were painted in soft shades of yellow, green, pink, blue and purple. There were many shade trees and even a few tree-lined streets as reminders of past British and Italian influence in this corner of east Africa.

My arrival in Kassala coincided with the start of Ramadan, the annual month-long dawn-to-dusk Muslin fast. Until I'd been there several days, I thought there were no restaurants, teashops or drink vendors in the entire city. In actual fact, there were two or three decent restaurants and dozens of small juice stands. During Ramadan, none opened for business until sunset.

I remember the first time I ventured into the *souk* during Ramadan. It looked like the Paris of eastern Sudan had come under a poison gas attack or had been struck by an outbreak of sleeping sickness. Almost everyone was asleep. Those who weren't were barely moving. People were asleep in doorways, on the floors and on the counters in their shops, propped up against each other, stretched out on the ground under trees. This was not altogether surprising. Temperatures were about 110-115 daily and one is not allowed to take even sips of water during daylight hours, if properly observing the Ramadan fast.

Crowds formed quickly around the teashops and juice stalls as soon as night fell. Cold juice drinks, made in blenders with ice water, sugar and your choice of orange, grapefruit, guava or mango juice, were only 25 piasters (eight cents) each. With temperatures and thirsts running so high, that seemed like the bargain of a lifetime. I tried hard to overlook the risk of hepatitis, as the glasses were rinsed but never properly washed between one customer and the next.

There were two restaurants we particularly liked and sometimes visited on Sundays, our cook's day off. One was a nameless sandwich shop, where we often bumped into some of our Eritrean friends and other *khawaja* relief workers. Spicy egg or meat sandwiches cost 75 piasters each there.

The open-air rooftop restaurant at the Palace Hotel was a little classier. We sometimes went there on special occasions. One night 11 of us went together because we'd heard the U.S. Information Service had sent a video of recent TV network news broadcasts. We'd heard the USIS provided this service periodically and thought we might see it on the hotel television set. This turned out to be nothing more than a rumor.

Nevertheless, we had an interesting meal on top of a very quaint four-story hotel. It appeared the hotel had been built without the advice of an architect. It looked like the builders had made it up as they went along. You almost got dizzy walking up the stairs. Everything was painted in lovely pastel shades. There were linen tablecloths and napkins on the tables. There was no menu, however, and no choice of food. Eating there was like going back to one's childhood; you got whatever Mom served. The first time we went, the main course was pigeon. Some in the group never returned for another meal at the Palace.

There were two movie theaters in Kassala. The movies were usually Egyptian or Indian, although there was an occasional American or British film. There was a different movie every night. Hand-lettered posters advertising each night's film were in Arabic, so we never really knew what was showing until we got there.

Once, we thought we were going to a Charlton Heston film. The theater owner wanted to let us in free to express his appreciation for our volunteer work. We'd have gladly paid the regular ticket price, 85 piasters or less than 30 cents, but he insisted. We gratefully accepted his offer.

The movie was not quite what we expected. Charlton Heston wasn't in it, but it was called *Charleston*. It was in English, but it was a bad film about bumbling art thieves trying to make off with a Gauguin from the Tate Gallery in London.

The movie theater itself was as interesting as the rooftop restaurant at the Palace Hotel. All seats were reserved. Ours were pale blue metal deck chairs, located in the back two rows, sitting unevenly on a concrete floor. All seating was enclosed within a corrugated metal fence. There was no roof over the theater. It was like going to a drive-in movie in a convertible with the top down, except the seats were wobbly and decidedly less comfortable than car seats.

The whole experience was delightful, despite the discomfort, the B-grade movie, the primitive sound system and out-of-focus French and Arabic sub-titles that covered the lower third of the screen. However, it was not a huge disappointment when 45 minutes into the movie, severe lightning and heavy rain forced everyone to get up and go home.

The next time we went to the movies, we went to the other open-air theater in town to see an Indian film with Arabic and English sub-titles. It was a love story between two men, one of whom was depressed because he had just lost his job. In one particularly bizarre scene, the two principal characters rode their bicycles along a beach while singing a love song to each other. Camels and a donkey-drawn cart passed in the background as they sang, while a token black man did a Caribbean dance. It was so bad it was hilarious. Once again, we left early. This time, the film broke and we'd reached the limits of our tolerance for sitting in uncomfortable chairs.

Movies were immensely popular with the Sudanese and the few Eritrean men who had settled in Kassala, even if we didn't fully appreciate them. We never saw a woman at a movie though, except volunteers from Kassala-based relief agencies.

Some nights, people were so anxious to get in the theaters that police were on duty to control the crowds. It appeared their mission was to prevent people from cutting in line or having friends already in line buy tickets for them. Punishment of violators was swift and severe. Policemen carried leather whips and, without offering warnings, walked up behind violators and lashed them across their backs. The night of the Indian movie, we saw a man running down the street to avoid a full whipping. Two uniformed policemen were in close pursuit.

Busses were the most common form of long-distance transport in Sudan, even though there were no actual bus stations.

Muslims at Wad Sherife refugee camp turned towards Mecca five times a day in prayer.

A refugee weaves two mats together during construction of the cholera isolation hospital at Wad Sherife.

All structures in the refugee camp were built from crude poles, mats, wire and rope.

An Eritrean refugee at work making a bed from ropes and poles. Note holes in the center of beds in background to accommodate cholera patients.

Irish nurse Mary Bowe with an Eritrean co-worker at a feeding center.

Paved roads were few and far between in Sudan. Here a truck crosses the desert between Kassala and Wad Sherife.

A vegetable seller in the Kassala market

Josef, an Eritrean artist, painted signs such as this one outside a feeding center at Wad Sherife.

Sadly, some refugees had to be given jobs as gravediggers at Wad Sherife.

Severe dust storms, or haboobs, sometimes blew through Kassala and the refugee camp at Wad Sherife.

Richard Leutzinger in the Wad Sherife classroom with one of his student medical examiners.

Pediatrician Karen Kruger with an Eritrean refugee child.

A refugee cook prepares food for children at a Wad Sherife feeding center.

Harry Belafonte interviews LARC physician Vic Snyder.

Shirley Cantrell, a nurse from Texas, with a refugee child.

Eritrean mother and child.

Flies in Sudan were an unspeakable nuisance. Here they cling to the tubing of a patient's intravenous infusion at the Wad Sherife inpatient clinic.

SIXTEEN

We were always searching for something new in the way of escape and entertainment. One morning at breakfast, someone suggested we get some cannabis. Splendid idea, several others agreed; why didn't we think of that sooner?

No one knew if such a thing existed in Sudan, where possession of alcohol was a serious crime. No one knew what the attitude was about drugs. Someone suggested we add cannibus to Gibrab's shopping list, along with the bread, tomatoes, bananas, grapefruit and whatever else he was to get today.

Gibrab went off to the *souk* at 7:00 in the morning, as was his usual custom. He needed to make two or three trips because he could carry only so much in the basket on the back of his bike, especially when watermelons were in season, as they were at this time.

Gibrab was gone his normal length of time, had completed the grocery shopping and also had found time to locate and buy what amounted to about two large handfuls of Sudanese cannibus or *bhango*. This had cost nine pounds, or less than three dollars of our grocery money. All we would need to find now would be some papers so we could roll up a few joints. None of us had brought any from home since almost none of us, it turned out, had even had a single smoke in the past several years. A few never had.

Bhango. What an appropriate word to describe something that just sneaks up on you from out of nowhere and goes bang! on your mind. It was just as good/just as bad as any cannibus on which I had lost my mind/expanded my mind during the few years leading up to 1970, which was the approximate time of my last smoke.

Someone was chewing on a piece of caramel while we listened to a tape of Chuck Mangione in the background. "If you close your eyes and listen to the music, you can see yourself chewing your caramel," he said. No one responded, until, moments later, someone suddenly began banging him on his back, asking if he was all right. He nodded weakly: no. He slumped forward in his chair, arms across his thighs. Someone said it looked like he was having difficulty breathing. Someone said to do a Heimlich maneuver on him. Was this really happening? Was this reality or an illusion? That's always the problem with drugs, isn't it? Separating reality from illusion?

Then people were picked up out of their chairs and moved by a power of which they were unaware, to do things without thought, as if mere instruments. Or they sat glued to their chairs, momentarily paralyzed, witnesses to a picture show. Picture show?

This was reality. The man in the chair slumped forward, unresponsive. Arms wrapped around him from behind, hand against fist against his stomach. Three upward thrusts were made, failing to evoke any response. Not a groan, not a whimper, not a gasp. Repeated thrusts were delivered with more power, with more authority, with a certain sense of urgency, as in "this is not a drill."

Every bit of the rescuer's strength was summoned. The fist was driven again and again and again, inwards and upwards against the stomach, against the diaphragm separating the stomach from the lungs, in an effort to free the caramel that was lodged in the man's upper airway like a wad of chewing gum stuffed in a bellows. Squeeze the bellows hard enough and you can shoot the gum across a room.

"Okay, stop."

It was the voice of the man in the chair. Suddenly, everyone knew he was all right. If air was able to pass upwards over the vocal cords so he could speak, it could pass downwards to supply oxygen to his lungs and body. If the man in the chair could speak, he would live.

The man who performed the Heimlich maneuver said later he could see this headline in the *National Enquirer*: **Relief Worker Chokes to Death During Wild Drug Party.**

The man in the chair was quiet for a few moments. Then, breathing easily, he said in a soft voice: "I think you just saved my life. I thought I was going to die."

The man who performed the Heimlich maneuver said after a few minutes of reflection: "I didn't feel any sense of panic, any rush of adrenalin. I didn't feel like you were going to die or like I was interfering with your death. I don't feel like I personally had anything to do with it. I was just an instrument that was picked up and moved to do what was done." After further reflection, he added: "It's good to know something you've been taught, and that you have taught, actually works."

The man in the chair didn't hear all that. He was lost deep in his own personal thoughts. He said simply, "I think I'll go to bed." Then he got up from his chair, disappeared down the garden path and went to bed.

The other man unwrapped another piece of caramel, put it into his mouth, made a mental note to be careful as he chewed and closed his eyes.

Next morning at breakfast, someone said to the man who almost hadn't been able to be there: "You know, it would have really ruined breakfast if we'd had to step over your body to get to the cornflakes this morning."

We never smoked *bhango* in Kassala again.

SEVENTEEN

Heretofore, the dirtiest job I ever had was working in a slaughterhouse one morning in Oregon in about 1961. I remember getting off for lunch, walking to my car, driving home and dropping my clothes in the garbage can before I went in the back door. I didn't go back to finish the day or collect my pay.

The cleanest jobs always have been as a nurse. I've usually had to dress completely in white—white shoes, white socks, white pants, white belt, white shirt. I've had weeks when I washed my hands so may times my skin dried up and the ends of my fingers split open.

On the 21st of June, I decided it was dirtier work being a nurse-teacher in Sudan than stacking hides in a slaughterhouse. On the 22nd of June, I decided I hadn't seen anything on the 21st. The 22nd was much dirtier than the day before.

June 21st is supposed to be the longest day of the year in the northern hemisphere, in terms of hours of daylight. The *haboob* or dust storm that descended on Kassala that day created a dim twilight two hours before sunset and made it a short day for us. At 4:00 p.m. the sky was its normal cloudless blue. By 4:30, it had turned a dark brownish-orange color and had blotted out the sun. By 5:00 o'clock we looked as if we'd just come out of a coal mine after a cave-in. We

91

were hot and sweaty from the 100-degree-plus temperature and the layer of dust that covered us had turned immediately to mud.

Some of the *haboob* stories that made the rounds among foreigners in Sudan were legendary. One time a LARC team got lost for two hours in a *haboob* on the drive from Kassala to Wad Sherife, which normally took half an hour. The dust was so thick that no navigational landmarks were visible. Headlights wouldn't penetrate the dust. No one had the faintest idea which direction to go. Finally, they had to stop, roll up the windows and wait for the sky to clear.

We had to interrupt my class for five minutes or so more than once while a dust storm blew through the classroom, undeterred by the thin palm mat walls. We all covered our eyes, noses and mouths with shirts, bandanas and in the case of one of my students, a turban, while we waited it out. Then we continued as if nothing had happened.

The worst *haboob* I saw blew through the hospital one morning, creating a dust cloud so thick you couldn't see the patients from one end of the ward to the other. I'll never forget the sight of Dr. Mike Schoenleber, dressed in t-shirt and shorts, with a red bandana covering his nose and mouth, examining patients as if everything was perfectly normal. Some afternoons we came home looking and feeling like we'd spent the day working inside a vacuum cleaner.

One day I forgot to close my suitcase before leaving Kassala for work. That was a mistake I made sure never to repeat. There was a *haboob* in Kassala that day. When I got home that afternoon, there was so much dirt in my suitcase it looked like someone had tried to bury it.

It rained the night of June 21 and early morning on the 22nd. It was the first rain of the year in this part of Africa. We knew precisely when the first drops fell. All of us who were sleeping outside had to get up and drag our beds inside.

Overnight, the streets of Kassala and the desert between there and Wad Sherife turned to thick, sticky, gooey mud. Anyone who had assumed the rain would be swallowed quickly by the sandy desert soil was reeducated during the drive to camp that morning. The soil was neither as sandy nor as absorbent as it looked. It was heavy clay called black cotton soil. It absorbed moisture very slowly and held it for a long time. When wet, it was like glue. It could suck your shoes off. It dried hard as concrete.

We followed the paved street across Kassala until it ended on the eastern edge of town that morning. Then we plunged into the first of many large puddles we would have to drive through on the way to Wad Sherife. As the four-wheel drive fishtailed through the first, a physical impossibility occurred. The muddy water thrown up from behind each wheel somehow was sucked into the vehicle through all the windows, front and back, left and right, bathing all of us in mud. If nothing else, an early morning mud bath gave us our first good laugh of the day. None of us could have survived our Sudan experience without an ability to laugh at ourselves, at our own shortcomings and peculiarities, at our daily setbacks and misfortunes, no matter how large or small.

It took us 90 minutes to drive roughly 10 miles to camp, three times as long as normal. We had to make up our route as we went along. At one point, we came to a small bridge that the day before had spanned only a low spot in the desert. Previously, I had thought this bridge was a humorous sight: a bridge in the middle of a barren desert, with no roads leading up to it and no water flowing beneath it. Now, we had to go through 20 yards of water before we could get onto the bridge to cross what presumably was deeper water.

Some vehicles without four-wheel-drive didn't make it through and got stuck in axle-deep water and mud. The passengers waded into the water to help push them out while the drivers raced there engines, spun their wheels and showered all the helpers with mud. Other vehicles made it through the water, got onto the bridge and then stalled. The only people who had an easy passage that morning were those on camels.

Finally, we arrived in camp to find disaster on top of disaster. The entire camp was a sea of mud. Not a single structure, from the smallest refugee *tukul* to the largest feeding center, was even remotely water repellent, since all were constructed of poles and mats. There was mud inside and out.

We had anticipated that it would rain eventually. We had tried to prepare the inpatient hospital by hanging heavy plastic sheets from the ceiling above the beds so the rainwater would be deflected away from the patients. However, some of the plastic sheets collected large amounts of water rather than deflecting it. When they became unable to bear more weight, they came unlashed from the ceiling and dumped the water on the patients. Then the runoff created mud holes in the middle of the hospital.

Even we couldn't find any humor in this pathetic situation. Here was a concentration of the 30 sickest refugees in a camp of 70,000 and our incompetence in protecting them from the rain had just added to their misery. When we arrived at about 8:30 that morning, all the patients were shivering cold. None had received their morning medications. Not a single one was receiving an IV infusion or being fed through a naso-gastric tube. All their tubes had come out during the night and it had been beyond the abilities of the two Eritrean medical assistants to replace them while working under such horrendous conditions.

The mud was so deep, thick and sticky that we had two choices about how to work in it. One, we could tie our shoes as tightly as possible and hope they wouldn't be sucked off. Two, those who wore sandals instead of shoes would have to go barefoot and hope they didn't step on anything sharp. Even the smallest puncture wound, if it became infected, could take months to heal.

We treated each of the 30 cold wet patients the same way. We picked up their beds, with the patients still on them if they were too sick to walk, and carried them out into the sun to dry off and warm up. An hour later, we had to carry them again to the shade of another shelter. The sun already had become too hot to bear.

We postponed my class that day so the students and I could spend the entire day working. Our classroom became a temporary hospital ward. I spent the day working with two students, giving medications, restarting IVs and reinserting naso-gastric tubes. I also put a catheter in an old man whose bladder had become painfully distended because he hadn't been able to urinate since the previous day.

At the same time, other nurses, medical assistants and students were playing musical chairs with beds. They moved beds and patients into the shade, back into the sun, back into the shade again. Vic Snyder was having a difficult time keeping track of whom he had seen and whom he hadn't during his daily examination of his patients. Adding to the chaos, one patient had a severe case of cerebral malaria and became delirious and combative. It took six of his family members and friends to keep him on his bed.

Even though we spent the entire day sloshing through ankle-deep mud, we were not allowed to forget this was an African desert, not far from the equator, on the second day of summer. The temperature was in the neighborhood of 110 degrees by midday.

Amazingly, not a single patient died during the night of rain or during the day that followed.

While one team of us spent the day with the patients, another was busy trying to salvage the inpatient building. All the patients would have to return to it by nightfall. Plastic sheeting was hung in a more efficient manner. A trailer load of sand was dumped at the entrance and spread by shovel and by hand to a depth of three or four inches over the entire floor, to cover the water and mud and absorb future rain.

I've always wished I had a photo of Susan Smith, barefoot medical director of the Lalmba-American Refugee Committee's relief program in Sudan, spreading sand over the muddy floor while on her hands and knees. It would be the perfect photo to show some whining worker, somewhere, some other time in life, who protested: "that's not my job…"

Ironically, 24 hours earlier and just hours before the big *haboob* and rain storm, Harry Belafonte had made a fact-finding visit to Wad Sherife with an entourage of 20 or 30 media people and photographers. They spent more then two hours there, asking questions, getting a first-hand look at the work being done and gathering information to help them decide how to distribute the millions of dollars raised by USA for Africa. By the day of the big rain, though, they were at some other camp, somewhere else in Sudan, totally unaware of our disaster on top of disaster.

EIGHTEEN

Each of us looked forward to working all night in the cholera isolation hospital with a mixture of feelings, both good and bad. Thinking about your next turn was like thinking about the funeral of an aging parent. The idea was almost too unpleasant to contemplate. Still, you knew that when the time came, you wouldn't miss being there for the world.

The admission rate and case load of cholera patients increased to the point where we needed two foreign-trained medical volunteers to work through each night with the Eritrean medical workers. While this guaranteed the night would be easier for each of the expatriates, it also meant our turns came around twice as often.

I had only to recall my experience the first night at the cholera hospital to know the next one would be so stressful and tiring that I wouldn't feel near normal again for days afterwards. At the same time, our *esprit de corps* was so strong that I truly wanted to do my part and spend another night there. My resolve to do another night and my apprehension about doing one rose each time I saw the others coming home from their night duty during the week preceding my turn.

Pediatrician Karen Kruger and Phena Cullen, a GOAL nurse from Ireland, had the bad luck to have worked the night of the first rain. Water poured onto them through the mat roof like it was passing through cheesecloth. Karen, Phena and everyone else were shivering cold by morning, an interesting phenomena in Sudan in mid-June. Karen was so cold her lips had turned blue. Only a few weeks before, her skin color had been orange and then greenish-yellow as she suffered through a severe bout of hepatitis and the jaundice that comes with it. Then, she was so sick she had no memory of her first week in bed. Yet she had such a burning desire to help the refugees, to make the best use of every minute of her time in Africa, she came to help at Wad Sherife on her days off from another LARC camp at Girba, about two hours to the southwest.

As if working through half the night in the rain hadn't been enough to bear, Karen and Phena were then forced to stay on until 11:00 o'clock the next morning before returning to Kassala for a shower and bed. There were no vehicles available to take then home. Every individual and every vehicle had been needed to deal with the effects of the year's first rain. A shortage of vehicles was a constant problem for the LARC team in Sudan.

Calm and stability had returned to the cholera hospital by two nights later. Marybeth McCarthy, a nurse from Massachusetts, and Mary Bowe, the other Irish nurse, had a fairly easy night. They worked through the night, were relieved early in the morning and set off in one of the Toyotas across the desert towards Kassala in anticipation of eating breakfast and getting to bed early. Then, they too met with a mishap.

Their vehicle became hopelessly mired in deep mud before getting halfway home. Try as they might, they couldn't get it out. Finally, they had to wade through hundreds of yards of mud and walk for more than an hour and a half across the desert—under the blazing sun, without water, after being on their feet for 24 hours—to get back to camp to find someone to help free their vehicle from the mud. They got home and to bed at 2:45 that afternoon.

Stress levels for the overnight staff were reduced significantly when the Swiss Red Cross managed to procure a generator and neon tube lighting for the isolation hospital. The task of safely monitoring as many as 50 IV infusions by lantern and flashlight had become almost impossible.

The first two to work nights with real lights were Shirley Cantrell, a former nun and now a nurse from Texas, and Vic Snyder, who usually chose to work all day, all night and then all day again without a break for sleep. Now, with lights and Shirley as a partner to work with, Vic actually found time for a rest break. During the middle of the night, he lay down on one of the rope beds in the staff *recubba* and fell sound asleep for half an hour. Lest no one would believe that Vic actually took a break, Shirley snapped a photo of him, eyes closed, stretched out, fully relaxed, sound asleep, with his stethoscope still in his ears.

We all feared that because of the rain, the cholera outbreak might turn into a full-blown epidemic. The cholera-causing organism, *vibrio cholera*, is passed from one person to another in water or food that has been contaminated by vomit or feces from an infected person. Prior to the rain, the characteristically watery stools and vomit quickly evaporated under the hot sun. After the rain, though, they became mixed with the mud and thousands of puddles of rainwater throughout the camp. The puddles were irresistible play areas for children. Inexplicably, there was no escalation in the number of cases following the rain. Admissions remained steady at about 30 a day.

Since the number of cases had stabilized, and because the addition of lights had made working nights so much easier, I decided to do my next turn of night duty without a partner. If we could do our nights one person at a time instead of in pairs, our turns to do them would come around only half as often. Everyone agreed that working one night every two weeks was preferable to one a week. Still, I had to turn down volunteers who wanted to stay up all night with me, in the middle of the desert in the heat of night, with over 100 patients suffering from diarrhea and vomiting.

You couldn't pay most people enough to do that kind of work, but there were always a few willing to do it for free. You don't think twice when your heart tells you it's the right thing to do.

NINETEEN

Working all night in the cholera hospital was not without its benefits. If you were there all night, you didn't have to drive home to Kassala in the afternoon. I decided fairly early on that the afternoon ride home ranked just behind the heat and diarrhea as my least favorite thing about being in Sudan. We all hated it.

It was difficult enough getting everybody together to leave from one house in Kassala at about 7:00 o'clock in the morning for the ride out to Wad Sherife. Some days, trying to round everyone up to return home was just short of impossible.

We had three vehicles. The Toyota pickup comfortably seated three but often carried 15. A Toyota Land Cruiser had seats for six but regularly carried a dozen or more. Lastly, there was a jeep-style Toyota that couldn't seat anyone comfortably. It generally carried eight or nine on the afternoon run to Kassala. We never went anywhere with a vehicle that was not overloaded. We filled each to capacity with LARC *khawajas* and then usually packed in a few more Eritreans we saw along the way between Wad Sherife and Kassala.

The vehicles left the two LARC houses where we lived in Kassala each morning as they were filled. One from each house was usually underway by 7:15 at the latest and the third picked up the stragglers from both. If only coming home had been so simple.

There was no official or even recognized time to stop work at Wad Sherife. Temperatures were so high and energy levels so low by 3:00 o'clock, though, that there was little point in staying later than that. Many days, we didn't last that long. The signal to stop work was when we became too hot to function physically and too tired to think straight. By then, we also were hungry, thirsty and becoming dehydrated because we'd exhausted our supplies of drinking water.

Worst of all, we were scattered all over the camp, in two or three different hospitals and clinics, in three feeding centers and who-knew-where in between. It seemed like there was always one person who couldn't be found or one who wasn't quite ready to go. And by the time he or she was ready, someone else was tied up and needed to stay a little longer. Sometimes there were eight people ready to head home and no vehicle was available.

One person, a Swiss lady named Heidi, almost always finished her work before anyone else. Unfortunately, she had the least patience for those who worked the longest. She was at Wad Sherife in a non-medical function. Those most likely to stay late were a doctor seeing a patient who had just been admitted, or a nurse reporting off to the evening workers at the cholera hospital. Everyone but Heidi understood and was at least outwardly patient about delays. We were not always patient with her impatience. Few angry words were ever exchanged between any of us, but there was occasionally some sniping at this time of day. Once, I lost my temper and shouted at Heidi, making her cry. I was remorseful for the rest of the day.

We each had an opinion about how many Eritreans could be packed into a vehicle without actually suffocating anyone on the ride home across the desert. The discomfort of riding over the bumpy desert while packed tightly together in extreme heat is beyond anyone's ability to imagine. The agony was magnified if you were riding in the back of a vehicle without padded seats.

It was punishing. It didn't matter how careful the driver was.

There was no speed slow enough to prevent the jolts of pain you received each time the vehicle dropped into another pothole. When that happened, your body became temporarily airborne and then crashed down against the metal wheel well or bed of the truck. I can't remember doing many things in my lifetime so physically abusive to my body.

It was amazing the vehicles could take such a fierce pounding without being shaken to pieces. The heat, dust and lack of roads did eventually take their toll, though. Spare parts were difficult if not impossible to obtain. Repairs took a long time and rarely restored a vehicle to its original condition. The deterioration of each vehicle was rapid and continuous.

Outsiders probably think that doctors and nurses do most of the work during famine relief efforts. However, none of their work would be possible if they couldn't get from one place to another and there were no vehicles to transport supplies. LARC was wise to this fact, of course, and sent first Rick Cheney and later David Schmidt from Minnesota with the primary responsibility of keeping our vehicles running.

Even buying gas was a difficult, time-consuming operation most of us would have found difficult to perform. Early on during his stay in Sudan, Rick had to travel to Port Sudan to buy a number of 55-gallon steel drums to store our gasoline in. Then, he had to go to an oil refinery to have them filled with gas. Eventually, he drove the volatile stash of fuel back to Kassala, where it was siphoned with a hand pump from the drums to each of our vehicles as needed.

The importance of Rick and David to our team could not be overstated. I don't recall a single breakdown during my three months at Wad Sherife and Kassala, although we averaged a flat tire every two or three days.

Unfortunately, the pickup was nearly totaled when hit by a Sudanese lorry one afternoon near camp. Fortunately, no one was hurt because that would have spoiled the comedy of the sequence of events that followed the crash.

The crash was unquestionably the fault of the Sudanese driver.

He was driving on the wrong side of the desert. He came around the corner of a building and smashed almost head-on into Carolyn Smith, who was driving the pickup. The Sudanese driver apparently got his bribe money to the police in Kassala before Carolyn arrived there. He was not held for questioning. The blame was going to be placed on her.

The police had no way of knowing what they would be up against if they tried to bully Carolyn. She had worked the previous seven or eight years as a Russian-English interpreter during the highest level Soviet-American talks in Geneva, Switzerland. She was also one of the first women in the world to have run a 26-mile marathon. She ran the Boston Marathon in the early seventies, when people were still discussing whether women should be allowed to enter. She did it because some friends at Brown University bet her a case of beer she couldn't. In short, Carolyn was an extremely bright, bold, witty, worldly and apparently fearless person. The police were overmatched.

They told Carolyn she was going to be arrested and detained. However, they told her she would have to sit down and wait a while before being arrested. It was Ramadan, the annual month-long dawn-to-dusk fast. The police had been fasting all day. It was now 6:00 o'clock in the evening, almost dusk. They were going to stop work and break their fasts, they told Carolyn. After they had a little something to eat and drink, they explained, in 30 minutes or an hour perhaps, they would arrest her, but not before.

Carolyn was not one to shrug her shoulders, utter the Sudanese word of ultimate resignation, *malesh*, and sit down to wait. An excellent linguist, she had become conversational in Arabic a short time after arriving in Sudan. She could speak to the police in Arabic or English, depending on whether she wanted them to understand or not. She told them in Arabic she would not wait, that she was leaving because she also wanted to break her fast. She told them in English to go fuck themselves if they didn't like it. Then she turned and walked out of the police station before they realized what was happening.

The police didn't have a vehicle in which to go after her. The policeman they sent out to chase her had to get a ride in the back of a *boxie*, a collective-style pickup truck/taxi. First, he had to find one that was going the same direction she was. He caught up with her some distance down the street, where Carolyn literally buried him under a barrage of English-language epithets. A small crowd had gathered and some in it apparently understood everything Carolyn said. The crowd broke into laughter. Humiliated and overmatched, the police let Carolyn off without arresting her.

Nevertheless, we were now down to two vehicles. Fortunately, UNHCR was able to loan us a Land Rover that had been donated by Band Aid, the British rock stars' aid-to-Africa project that was the forerunner to the even more successful fund-raising projects, USA for Africa and Live Aid.

TWENTY

Driving on the paved road that linked Khartoum to Kassala to Port Sudan was a treat, relatively speaking, after the bruising daily trips to Wad Sherife and back. The modest little two-lane highway, connecting Sudan's capital city to its only seaport, was 700 miles long. Aside from a few city streets, it was the only paved road in the largest country in Africa, covering 966,757 square miles. That's roughly the area of all the United States between the Mississippi River and the Atlantic Ocean. Bob Enik was the only LARC volunteer who drove on it with any regularity, making periodic trips to Khartoum to pick up supplies. The rest of us had our memories and stories to tell, even if we had traveled it only once.

To describe the road as sub-standard would be over-rating it. Chinese had constructed one section of the road, Yugoslavs another and Germans still another, according to stories we heard. There was a clear difference in the quality of the surface from one section to the next.

Much of the road was in a state of deterioration, especially the side that carried trucks bringing all the country's imports from Port Sudan. Temperatures exceeding 120 degrees literally melted the road. The wheels of heavily overloaded trucks caused two ever-deepening parallel grooves along the lane of the road taking in-going traffic. The opposite lane was in reasonably good repair since most of the trucks headed toward Port Sudan were empty and weighed much less.

The deep foot-wide grooves down one side of the road made travel extremely dangerous, no matter which direction you were going. If you crossed from the right side of the road to the left to pass another vehicle while traveling on the good side of the road, your tires could drop into the grooves on the bad side. That left you traveling at a high speed directly into oncoming traffic, like a train on the wrong tracks. To break free, you had to turn overly sharply, taking the risk you might lose control and careen off the right side of the road.

Traveling at night increased the risks a hundredfold. There were a few spots where the road had disintegrated altogether and simply ceased to exist. One such stretch between Khartoum and Kassala was about 50 yards long. There were no warning signs as one approached in either direction. You simply, and suddenly, in the dark of night, dropped off the road onto the desert while going 50 miles an hour. Then, just as the shock of what had happened was being realized, you were jolted back up onto the pavement again.

Industrial-sized potholes were slightly less hazardous but only if both hands remained firmly on the steering wheel. I was nearly knocked unconscious once when our vehicle dropped into a major pothole and my head struck the ceiling of the cab.

The greatest danger of driving at night was the risk of encountering a disabled truck parked on the road. There was no off-road parking except at the occasional village or rest stop. The shoulder was too narrow, if and where one existed, to allow a truck to pull completely off the road. If a truck did leave the road completely and park on the desert, it might not be able to get back on, especially when loaded to capacity. The roadbed was elevated too high above the desert. Trucks were rarely equipped with reflectors or other devices to warn oncoming traffic they had broken down. If you came upon a disabled truck in the night and at the same time were temporarily blinded by the headlights of an approaching vehicle, a crash was inevitable.

Both Lalmba and ARC eventually banned their people from driving on the road at night, except in cases of extreme emergency. We heard stories of *khawajas* from other relief agencies who were killed or badly injured as a result of after-dark collisions with disabled trucks.

I traveled the road at night twice: once as we returned from a party in Girba, a second time while headed to my next assignment with Lalmba, following my final day with LARC. Although fully aware of the risk, I don't remember being the least bit scared. I had decided subconsciously that I was invincible. It was illogical to think of coming all the way to Sudan to get killed.

TWENTY-ONE

I made my decision to work all night as the lone medical *khawaja* in the cholera hospital because there had been less than 15 new admissions by 3:00 o'clock that afternoon, when the last vehicle was to drive back to Kassala. There were fewer than 15 patients receiving IV infusions. The Eritrean medical assistants had become more proficient at their jobs with each passing day. I felt I could depend on them for reliable support.

Besides, someone from Scholars Against Hunger, a group of American college students spending part of their summer working at Wad Sherife, would also be there to help. Although few of them had any medical training, they could help mix and pass out oral rehydration solution to moderately ill patients. They could pass out milk, tea and biscuits to recovering patients and the family member each had at his or her bedside to help with care. Another equally important task, but one that no one liked to think about: they could empty the bedside buckets of liquid vomit and diarrhea stool. It looked like a night I could handle as the sole expatriate medical person.

I didn't take a break at 3:00 o'clock to go back to Kassala for a shower and dinner, as I had the first time I worked the night shift. I worked my normal day, teaching a class in the morning and tutoring a student as he passed out medications in the inpatient clinic in the afternoon. I went straight from there to the cholera hospital. The rain had transformed much of the desert between Wad Sherife and Kassala into a swamp. The ride back and forth now took at least an hour each way, passing over such rough terrain in some places that you felt like you had been mugged before you reached your destination. I didn't fancy making two additional crossings in one afternoon as preparation for staying up all night. None of us did anymore. We all just ran day into night into morning without a break.

I did my rounds, seeing and assessing each of the 50 or so patients, as soon as I arrived at the cholera unit. With my Eritrean assistant acting as translator, we went up and down the four rows of beds, from patient to patient, looking at each chart, asking each patient about his diarrhea, vomiting and ability to pass urine and drink. We also checked everyone's pulse and a few blood pressures. With a stethoscope, we listened to the lungs of some patients to make sure they hadn't been overloaded with intravenous fluids. We adjusted the flow rate of each IV as we went along. We found some patients whose IVs needed restarting because the fluid was no longer infusing into a vein. We found others whose IV fluid containers were empty and needed replacing. Some IVs were discontinued because the patients no longer showed signs of dehydration. Along the way, we also found a few patients who needed additional medicines prescribed because they were showing signs and symptoms of other diseases or illnesses besides cholera. It took almost two hours to see and assess every patient.

After seeing everyone once, I decided I should reevaluate the sickest ones. There had been so many interruptions, though, that I couldn't remember which ones I wanted to see a second time. All I could do was start over and see the whole group again.

By the time I had completed my rounds a second time, I had admitted two new patients and transferred a few others out to the convalescent area, to create some bed space for middle-of-the-night emergencies. I'd also started an IV, diagnosed a child as having pneumonia and started her on antibiotics, and found a number of adults who needed to begin treatment for malaria.

Suddenly and almost simultaneously, my Eritrean assistants and I realized it might rain. The first warning was a *haboob* that filled the cholera *recubba* with clouds of thick dust. At one point, we could barely see from one end of the *recubba* to the other. Soon, we were witness to roaring claps of thunder and bolts of lightning. With each flash of lightning illuminating the night sky, we could see heavy clouds, not far off, in the direction from which the wind was blowing.

We were better prepared for the rain now than we had been before the first storm. We had three heavy canvas army tents, each with a capacity of about 25 beds, for emergency use. It would seem to make obvious good sense to keep everyone in the tents all the time, but it was unbearably hot inside them, even with the sides rolled up to let air circulate through. The dark green canvas seemed to attract heat like solar panels, even magnifying it. We couldn't even hang IV fluid containers from the ropes and poles supporting the tops of tents during the day because the solutions quickly became too hot to infuse into the patients. Nevertheless, the tents were waterproof and just what we needed during the infrequent rainstorms.

After a brief period of deliberation, I decided we would move everybody from the *recubba* to the tents. It didn't occur to me to count the patients before moving them or to count the beds in the tents. Some of the patients were able to walk to the tents and did so, taking with them their few belongings and the family member staying with them. Each patient had one person staying him (or her), to help wash and feed him and empty his buckets of vomit and feces. No one was allowed more than one family member, though, because of the risk that that person would become infected. The companion received prophylactic treatment against cholera in the form of tetracycline capsules.

We carried most of the non-ambulatory patients from the *recubba* to the tents on stretchers or plastic sheets. In a few cases, we picked up an entire bed with the patient on it and walked to one of the tents.

Everyone fit into the two tents that were equipped with lights, but just barely. We had to place some of the beds within a foot of the next one. After everyone had been moved, we found there wasn't a single vacant bed for an emergency admission later in the night. It was imperative to have a few empty beds. We had to find a few people to vacate their beds. Again, we assessed the patients, one by one, until we found a few who had stabilized enough to be transferred to the convalescent area. Space there was more or less unlimited because the patients sat or lay on mats on the ground. Their treatment consisted of nothing more than tetracycline capsules, given three times a day, and all the ORS they could drink.

Cholera is a volatile disease. Without treatment, a person can die of dehydration within a few hours. However, if diagnosed quickly and given a few liters of intravenous fluids, most recover rapidly.

We also discovered during our rounds that a few of the beds were occupied by people who weren't sick and never had been. During the move from *recubba* to tents, a few of the patients' family members had claimed beds for themselves. Who was to know the difference? Patients aren't issued hospital gowns or identification bracelets in refugee camp hospitals. They wear the same thing during their hospitalization as they were wearing when they came in. In sickness or in health, they looked pretty much the same. By the time we had finished our rounds a fourth time, weeding out rapidly recovering patients and misplaced family attendants, we had created several empty beds for middle of the night admissions.

In the midst of this chaotic reshuffling, the Eritrean medical assistants on the 2:00-to-10:00 o'clock shift went home. Another group that would work from 10:00 p.m. to 7:00 a.m. replaced them. The new workers were all strangers to me. They came from the Swiss Red Cross team and brought with them four more new names to remember: Aklilu, Rafael, Asafau and Mohammed Ali. I wrote their names with a ballpoint pen on the palm of my left hand and hoped I could memorize them before repeated hand washings made them unreadable.

There was also a fifth arrival, from the LARC team, who Susan Smith had given me instructions to fire when he came to work. His patient assessment skills were too poor and his experience too limited to be able to give safe care without extremely close supervision. I had never fired anyone before, although I'd been fired from a few jobs myself. Both he and I found the experience extremely upsetting. Both of us were close to tears. This, understand, was over a job that paid him about four pounds a night, approximately $1.30. You can talk all you want about lost dignity, hurt pride and crushed feelings, but in the case of a refugee like this, the loss of income contributed largely to his upset. I paid him the money he had earned to date, consoled him as best as I could, and told him Susan might be able to find him another job, better suited to his skills and experience. I meant it sincerely. Fortunately, the very next day, Susan rehired him to do a non-medical job.

That emotionally traumatic experience out of the way, I turned to the next problem. Wind was threatening to blow one of the tents away. It was a toss-up as to whether it would be lifted off the ground or would collapse inward on everyone inside. In fact, at almost the exact same time we were out in the howling wind and swirling dust of the *haboob*, driving in new tent stakes along the windward side of the tents, a similar tent at LARC's hospital for non-cholera patients actually did blow down. The patients there had to be moved from under the collapsed waterproof tent back to the sieve-like *recubba*.

By 1:00 o'clock in the morning, only 10 hours after I'd started my shift at the cholera hospital, I finally felt everything was under control. I'd learned the names of my assistants. The tent was once again staked and tied securely to earth. All the bed-ridden patients were under canvas, safe from the rain. No one was on a bed who didn't belong on one. And there were empty beds ready for new cases, should any be admitted during the night.

We even had the bonus of an extra helper from Scholars Against Hunger. The van that was supposed to bring Leamon Abrams from Kassala to work from 10:00 p.m. to 7:30 a.m. and take Andy Rusk back home got stuck in the mud coming through the banana plantation two miles from the hospital. Leamon walked the two miles through mud and darkness to get to work. Andy was stranded with us for the night. I was glad to have them both.

111

Andy mixed 10-gallon batches of oral rehydration solution as the barrels ran dry. He made frequent rounds of the patients to refill their cups and urge them to drink more ORS. He helped us move the patients, their beds and belongings when we decided it was going to rain. He worked cheerfully, as if he was on the greatest adventure of his life. Finally, in the early hours of the morning, he collapsed exhaustedly onto the rope bed next to the generator in the staff rest area and fell fast asleep.

Leamon, who only a month before had been awarded his master's degree in city and regional planning from Harvard, spent the night assisting two young Eritrean women, a cook and a cleaner. He helped the cook distribute the midnight and early morning rations of milk, tea and high-energy biscuits to the patients and family in both tents and in the convalescent *recubba*. After the midnight snack had been passed out, he spent the next several hours helping the cleaner in the most unenviable of jobs. They collected, emptied and redistributed the buckets for catching vomit and diarrhea stool that had been left behind during the transfer of patients to the tents. The young woman working with Leamon found the job so distasteful that she vomited four times herself during the night. At one point, she had to stop work, sit down and cry before she could continue.

At 1:30 in the morning, I decided to go into the staff *recubba* and lie down. I was so tired physically and so drained emotionally that I didn't even hear the diesel-powered generator, three feet from my head. I fell asleep immediately. I slept for 45 minutes, until something bit me on the neck. I was immediately so wide awake and so refreshed that I got up and went back to the tents, where I spent the rest of the night.

By daybreak, we had admitted about 15 new patients. We had to start an IV infusion on every one of them, but since we had lights this was not difficult.

The rain never came. At 6:00 o'clock we began moving the patients from the tents back to the *recubba*. At 7:00 o'clock, Aklilu, Rafael, Asafau, Mohammed Ali, the cook and the cleaner were replaced by a new group of Eritrean refugee workers. Almost simultaneously, a Norwegian doctor named Eigel (I've forgotten his last name) from the Swiss Red Cross arrived to do his rounds of the patients while I gave him a report on each one's condition and progress.

That was my intent, anyway. We had just moved approximately 50 patients and 50 family members from two tents into one *recubba*. I was totally confused. I could neither remember nor recognize which were the sickest. In several cases, I couldn't tell which of the two people sitting on a bed was the patient and which was the supporting family member. And what had happened to the child I had diagnosed with pneumonia along with her cholera? Where did she go? We never found her. The Eritrean medical assistants that had just come to work were of no help except as translators when Eigel or I wanted to question a patient. They had never seen most of these patients before. I felt as if I hadn't either.

I wondered during the ride home to Kassala if Eigel thought I was as stupid as I felt. If he did, he never let on.

TWENTY-TWO

The human being is a marvelously adaptable creature. When I thought about it later, I decided I'd done a decent job the night before in the cholera hospital. I'd reacted and adapted as I'd needed to. I'd coped. And I could still see the lighter side of working such long hours under such horrendous conditions for nothing.

I wrote a letter to Hugh and Marty Downey in Colorado to reiterate my thanks for having recruited me, hiring me and giving me such a good orientation before sending me out to Sudan. "I have some ideas about how you might make the orientation even more meaningful, to even better prepare people," I told them. "The night before they begin, fill them up with prune juice and Milk of Magnesia. Then early next morning, at say 5:15, get them up and put then into a pre-heated sauna, in which you also have heated and spread over the floor individual helpings of camel shit, donkey shit, goat shit, horse shit, dog shit and human shit. Then you put on the videos, right there in the sauna, showing volunteers working in a refugee camp, okay? Then, after about three hours, you bring in a vacuum cleaner, throw it into reverse, push the ON button, yell "*haboob*" and empty it out right there in the sauna.

"You'll then have everybody right where you want then. Tell

them if they meet your qualifications and you decide you like them well enough, you'll be willing to give them non-paying jobs and they'll only have to pay part of their plane fares to get there. How will anyone be able to turn you down? Your recruiting success rate should go up by 100 percent."

* * *

My training and work as a nurse in Britain in the early seventies probably did more to prepare me to work at Wad Sherife than anything I read or that anyone could have told me. British-trained nurses often are more innovative and adaptable than those trained in America, where there is some device or piece of equipment to help complete most every task or procedure. American-trained nurses are also accustomed to using something once and throwing it away. I liked the idea of having to create one piece of equipment from the remains of another, or using things over and over until they were truly worn out.

If you want the head of a patient's bed elevated in an American hospital, you push a button and the head of the bed goes up. In Britain, in the days when I worked there, you'd tuck several pillows in behind the patient's head, neck and shoulders. One day at Wad Sherife I saw an old man in heart failure. Fluids accumulating in his lungs would have drowned him if we had not been able to sit him upright in his crude rope bed. We dug two small holes, into which we placed the legs of the foot of the bed, making it lower. We placed bricks under the legs at the head of the bed, raising that end. Then we made a large wedge from a discarded cardboard carton, covered it with a blanket and put that between the bed and head and shoulders of the old man. With little more than our ingenuity, we managed to get him up to almost a 90-degree angle.

If a patient complains of being too warm in an American hospital, one of the nurse's first reactions might be to adjust the thermostat in the patient's private room. A British nurse would be more likely to open a window. At Wad Sherife, there were times when someone took a pair of scissors or a knife and cut a hole in the mat wall, at once creating a window and increasing air circulation.

Supplies were so limited and difficult to obtain that almost nothing was thrown away. An empty penicillin vial became a container for a sputum specimen that needed to be examined in the laboratory. If we didn't use an entire bag of intravenous fluid on one patient, the remainder went into another. IVs were hung from the ceiling or from the stubs of branches on the crude poles that supported the walls. An empty IV bag and tubing became the naso-gastric feeding apparatus for another patient. We cut a hole in the top of the fluid container so it could be filled with milk and we removed the needle from the end of the tubing so it could be safely passed through the patient's nose and throat and down to his stomach. We also used empty IV bags and tubing as the drainage collection units and the end of urinary catheters.

Disposable single-use plastic syringes and steel needles, commonly used for giving injections in both Britain and the United States, were used multiple times at Wad Sherife. We rinsed them and then sterilized them in a common kitchen pressure cooker that we heated over a small kerosene burner. We used these needles and syringes over and over and over again. We threw them away, reluctantly, when the needles became so dull they would no longer penetrate human skin or when all the calibrations had worn off the syringes.

We couldn't even wash our hands without a great deal of improvisation. Water was brought from Kassala to Wad Sherife daily in tank trucks and placed in a number of storage tanks scattered around the refugee camp. It was carried from there into the hospitals and outpatient clinics by bucket or by garden hose and placed in cisterns. The cisterns were made of oil drums that had been cut in half and had brass taps affixed to their bottoms. A large pan or another bucket was placed beneath the tap to catch the water coming out of the tap and passing through our hands as we washed. That pan or bucket of dirty water had to be hand-carried outside and dumped frequently, for any overflow or spillage onto the dirt floor would turn the hospital into a mud hole and breeding area for mosquitoes.

The masters of creativity and adaptability were the refugees and the Sudanese. The refugees had built their *tukuls* and their beds from nothing more than sticks and poles, mats, rope and wire.

Blacksmiths who made knives, swords and various farming tools from springs and other old auto parts occupied an entire section of the *souk* in Kassala. Craftsmen who made cooking utensils out of old tin cans occupied another section. They made pots, pans and even portable charcoal fireplaces that were not unlike Japanese hibachis.

Commercially manufactured toys are an unheard of luxury in a country as poor as Sudan. A clever father, though, could turn an empty one-gallon can into a marvelous truck for his son, using only a crude cutting tool and his ingenuity. These trucks were invariably fitted with wheels made of discs cut from worn-out soft-rubber flip-flop sandals. There was one merchant in the *souk* that sold sandals made from old tires. Several others dealt in useful, practical, sturdy handbags made from old sugar sacks. Nothing got wasted.

TWENTY-THREE

Teachers in the United States would give anything to have students as highly motivated and well disciplined as those I had at Wad Sherife. They made me think of Abe Lincoln, lying on the floor in front of the fireplace, trying to learn his spelling words in semi-darkness.

The 13 refugee students at Wad Sherife didn't have lights in their *tukuls* since there wasn't any electricity. They didn't have fireplaces either. They had to do all their studying between 5:30 and 7:30 in the morning—that is, between sunrise and the start of classes—or between 2:30 and 6:30 in the afternoon. The afternoons, between the end of the workday and sunset, were hours of the day when temperatures were highest and human energy lowest. Some days they had even less study time available because they had to begin work at the clinic at 7:00 a.m. or had to work until 10:00 p.m. in the cholera unit. Once a week, each of them also had to work a 24-hour shift in the hospital.

There were few complaints. Almost no one ever missed a class. For every student in our training program, there were at least two others who wanted to take part. Almost every day, someone asked for a copy of our textbook, *Where There Is No Doctor*. Our classroom was surrounded by a protective barrier of dried thorn bushes, the African equivalent of barbed wire, to prevent the distraction of outsiders leaning in through the windows during every class.

The students had an insatiable thirst for learning. Once, Kubrom Humed spent his night off in Kassala. He got up at sunrise the next morning and walked two hours across the desert to Wad Sherife to get to class on time. Another student showed up for class on a Sunday morning, even though it was his day off and unbeknownst to him, it was the one day of the week we didn't have a class. He told me on Monday it had been worthwhile coming in anyway. He had gotten to deliver a baby.

It's impossible to gauge the difficulty the students must have had getting through their assignments. Our copies of *Where There Is No Doctor* were printed in English, which was no one's native language but mine. Zemuy Ghebremeskel had been a teacher in Eritrea and spoke seven languages, but even he was unable to read through every assignment without having to look up the meaning of a few words now and then. Ghebrehiwet Habte, the least skilled linguist of the students, was delighted to get through an entire paragraph without referring to the glossary in the back of the book.

After the first weekly written examination, on which scores ranged from Tesfomichael Bahta's 80 percent to Ghebrehiwet's 27, I decided all future exams would be open book. Although the scores might be artificially high, this would make taking each exam a learning experience. Besides, I wanted everyone to get used to using *Where There Is No Doctor* as a reference book. This was especially important for those diagnosing and treating people in the outpatient clinics. I told them it wasn't important to remember how many milligrams of tetracycline to give a child with cholera if you can find the dosage in the book. Any medical practitioner who tries to remember everything and treat every case without occasionally using a reference book is a dangerous practitioner.

Imagine my surprise when the scores on the second week's exam were only slightly higher than the first's. Why didn't they do better on an open-book exam than they had without using their books? I was puzzled. We discussed this at length. Eventually, I realized that most didn't have the faintest idea how to use the table of contents or index of the book. If they were unable to thumb through the pages to find what they wanted, they were unable to find it at all. Scores improved remarkably the third week, following a lesson on how to use the book.

This was only one of several occasions on which I completely misjudged the skills, abilities and needs of the students. Most had 11th or 12th grade educations. Everyone spoke English, although a few so poorly it was a constant handicap to their learning. Everyone had some previous medical training, usually basic anatomy and physiology in school science classes. A few had some informal but practical on-the-job learning as field medics during the civil war. Because some could perform sophisticated procedures such as spinal taps and wound suturing, I overlooked the fact they might know nothing of the very basics of giving safe care and treatment.

For example, I thought I did a thorough job of teaching how to prepare a needle and syringe and cleanse a person's skin, to prevent introducing an infection when giving an injection. We went through the steps of washing one's hands, using a disinfectant to clean the area of the skin to be injected, and loading the syringe with medicine without contaminating the needle, syringe or medication. They all demonstrated their proficiency. We even practiced giving injections of sterile saline to each other. It wasn't until sometime later, while watching a student insert a needle into the vein of a cholera patient, that I realized I'd failed to tell them some things they should not do. I hadn't told them not to blow on a patient's arm to dry off the disinfectant. I hadn't told them they shouldn't wipe away excess disinfectant with their shirttails or the heel of their hand.

I was surprised to find that almost no one knew how to calculate medication doses, although they had all been going through the motions. Few could figure out that if you wanted to treat someone with a particular medicine, at a dose of X number of milligrams per day for each kilogram of the patient's body weight, divided into four equal daily doses, you simply multiplied the number of milligrams times the number of kilograms and divided by the number of doses. They were equally baffled by trying to figure out how much liquid had to be drawn into a syringe to give an injection of 250,000 units of penicillin, if a vial containing 5,000,000 of penicillin powder had been reconstituted with five milliliters of sterile water.

Calculating correct medication doses is such an obvious high priority in giving safe care and treatment that solving a problem together became the first part of every lesson, every day, through the first two months of classes. My most satisfying accomplishment in Sudan was getting every student to the point where he could safely mix and dispense medications.

Samuel Jamie lagged behind the others in grasping the concept of calculating correct doses. He was otherwise one of the best students. He had a kind, caring bedside manner unsurpassed by that of anyone I've worked with in the health care profession anywhere. We spent one-on-one sessions together. I saw the other students and medical assistants trying to help Samuel. He just couldn't understand. Then one day we suddenly realized why. Samuel could add, Samuel could subtract, Samuel could multiply, but he couldn't divide. Somehow this skill had eluded him at school in Eritrea.

The problem was no sooner discovered than it was solved. Ross Tannebaum, a physician from Chicago who had arrived in Wad Sherife not long before, gave Samuel a solar-powered pocket calculator. He learned to use it almost immediately. What had seemed an insurmountable problem one day, which might have prevented Samuel from doing the work for which he otherwise seemed so eminently suited, was no longer a problem by the next day.

Sometimes the problem wasn't how little the students knew but how little I knew. Our classes placed the most emphasis on the recognition, treatment and prevention of the diseases most common to this part of Africa. Foremost in that category was malaria. Malaria kills more than 1,000,000 people a year in Africa. Malaria has killed more people than all the wars in history together. All but one of my students had had malaria, some several times. I didn't know a single American who had ever had malaria. I had never seen a case, although I eventually would become one myself.

Tuberculosis, polio, measles and whooping cough, diseases that are seldom seen in the more developed countries of the world because of immunization programs, were other diseases that I had to learn about as well as teach.

One person with a problem unique among the students was Manna Gebru. She had to stop attending classes to have a baby. Manna and her husband Gehbru, a gentle and refined man who had been a judge in Eritrea, lived in a mud house on the edge of Kassala. They had been there since fleeing the civil war years before. Since we passed within half a mile of their house every day on the way home from camp, I stopped off twice a week and gave Manna the same lectures I'd given at Wad Sherife. She continued with her reading assignments, studied and took her weekly exams at home.

She benefited from the individual attention since she didn't understand English particularly well. At the same time, I got to be with an Eritrean family in their home twice a week. I was never allowed to leave without having coffee with Manna and Gehbru, sometimes shared a meal with them and attended a party celebrating the third birthday of their son Gigi. The party was remarkably similar to birthday parties in the United States and Britain, right down to blowing out the candles, one for each year.

TWENTY-FOUR

Dr. Ross Tannebaum was fortunate to get to Sudan to do volunteer work with refugees. He could have as easily been a hostage in Lebanon. He traveled from the United States on one of five Trans World Airlines flights that would land that June day in Athens, completing the first leg of his journey to Africa. Four of the five TWA planes landed and took off again without incident. Terrorists boarded the fifth and forced it to fly to Beirut. Ross, luckily, was on a plane that flew safely to Egypt, where he spent several days exploring the pyramids and Nile, before realizing how close he had come to being highjacked.

It was interesting to speculate about how Ross might have dealt with his captors, had he been highjacked. Ross immersed himself so deeply into whatever he was doing that he sometimes appeared totally unaware of what was going on around him. It took only a slight stretch of the imagination to believe that if Ross had been concentrating on something else at the time, he might not have even noticed he'd been highjacked.

Ross began every morning in Kassala the same way. Shortly after waking up, he walked down the garden path to the shower at the far end of the house. He was not the earliest riser, so the shower was often in use when he got there. Still, day after day, with absolute predictability, Ross would try to open the door to the shower, knock when it wouldn't open and then ask: "Is anybody in there?" The question always made me respond silently: No, Ross. The last person to take a shower left the door locked, the water running and climbed out the window.

After eventually having his shower and eating a bowl of Egyptian cornflakes, Ross moved on to his daily shaving ritual. Ross had the brilliance to be a throat surgeon and street smarts to have survived as a Chicago taxi cab driver, but he was resolutely unable to shave without a mirror. Being well over six feet tall, he had to kneel to see himself in the little mirror he balanced on the back edge of a sink. We sometimes wondered what he saw in it. Once, he walked into the hospital at Wad Sherife with shaving cream in his ears and on his neck, his towel around his neck, and his stethoscope draped over the towel.

In fairness to Ross, he might have awakened each morning and immediately began thinking of what he could do that day to improve the care we were giving to the refugees.

Almost from the day he arrived, Ross worked to improve and expand the laboratory, which in developed countries plays a huge role in the diagnosis of diseases. Before his arrival, our lab consisted of one Eritrean lab technician, Yamani, and one monocular microscope, set up by a window in a corner of the outpatient clinic. The microscope was of toyshop quality and sophistication. It worked only when it could receive and reflect sunlight up through the specimen being examined. The lab could not operate on days when rain, clouds or a *haboob* blocked the sun from coming through the window.

Ross also located an x-ray technician at the Sudanese hospital in Kassala who would do chest x-rays on our patients for as little as one Sudanese pound each, approximately 30 cents. Almost every week thereafter, a carload of Eritrean patients was sent to the hospital in Kassala for x-rays, financed by Ross.

Ross also discovered the Eritrean Red Cross and Red Crescent

Hospital, a surgical hospital that, unbeknownst to the rest of us, was performing about 1,500 surgeries a year on Eritreans. The surgeons were all Egyptians and, like us, deeply committed to serving refugees. Zaki Moustafa El Sayei, head of the surgical team, was on his second tour of duty in Sudan. He had already spent four years operating on needy refugees in Kassala and Port Sudan, where the Egyptians staffed a second surgical hospital. They happily added to their caseload any patients from our hospital that needed surgery.

Although Ross was a surgeon, he was rarely able to perform a surgery in Sudan. We didn't have the equipment needed to run an operating room or a suitable room. Everything in Wad Sherife had been built by covering crude pole frames with mats, which were no barrier whatsoever against a dust storm. It would have been unthinkable to open a patient's abdomen when there was the ever-present risk of a *haboob*. A belly full of dirt would mean certain death.

The Eritrean Red Cross and Red Crescent Hospital was constructed of mud bricks, had shuttered windows and a roof which was impenetrable to both dust and rain. It had electricity most of the time. Electricity was necessary for the obvious reason that surgeons don't work well in the dark. Almost as important, electricity was needed to power the fans. Strategically placed fans kept flies from landing inside the patients and on sterile instruments. Flies were unspeakable nuisances. Ross was doing a spinal tap at Wad Sherife one day when a fly landed on the tip of the sterile needle he was using, just as he was about to insert it into a child's spinal column. Flies didn't like wind, though, and would not settle in front of a fan.

Fans also helped cool the Egyptian surgeons, Zaki and Atif Abd. El Azim. They needed to swathe themselves in sterile gowns and gloves so they wouldn't contaminate of their patients. They did ignore another convention by not wearing masks. Had they done otherwise, they might have suffocated in the heat. Fouad Hassan, the anesthesiologist, was not such a threat to contaminate the patients since he never touched their open wounds. He didn't wear a gown, gloves, mask or even a shirt.

Another problem the surgeons faced was diarrhea. Nobody was immune. A person might get lucky and go five or six days without diarrhea, but eventually he would have a day when he had to visit the latrine five or six times within a few hours. There was the chance, of course, that a surgeon might get the desperate urge while in the middle of a complicated case. A surgeon spends considerable time preparing himself for each case, scrubbing his hands and arms with antiseptic and then putting on the gown and gloves to create a sterile cocoon around himself. His concentration as he works must be trancelike. Imagine yourself in that position when, all of a sudden, oh, oh, oooh nooo…gotta go.

Electricity failures and diarrhea were mere inconveniences when measured against the biggest problem the Egyptians faced. They were always short of surgical supplies. They lived in constant fear that one day they would be unable to work because they had run out of sutures or some such thing.

Their fear was justified. They were not the beneficiaries of prolonged fund-raising drives at home or of such generous government grants as were many of the large, better-known relief agencies. When they ran out of something they particularly needed, they couldn't go scavenging the other refugee camps in eastern Sudan, as we often had to do. No one else was likely to have the specialized supplies they needed. No one else was doing surgery on refugees.

One evening over dinner, Zaki told us of the countless disappointments they had had when receiving shipments of supplies. They had received supplies rendered useless by the extreme heat, which were outdated or were simply inappropriate for their needs. Once, they received more than a ton of intravenous fluids, sent amidst a flurry of publicity by the Iraqi government. The fluids were of such a high concentration of dextrose in water that they couldn't be used for anything except making sweet tea.

We helped as best we could, always sending intravenous cannulas, fluids and antibiotics with every patient we sent them. Our help seemed terribly inadequate. It was miraculous the Egyptians could achieve so much when surgical and anesthetic supplies were so scarce. To this day, I am somehow more moved by the work they were doing than by what we did.

Egyptians aside, one of my everlasting memories will be of Ross as he performed one of his rare surgeries. If I close my eyes now, I can still see him kneeling on the dirt floor in the hospital at Wad Sherife, doing minor abdominal surgery on a fully-conscious woman lying on a rope bed. He had instructed an assistant to fan the open wound continuously as he worked to keep flies from landing in the sterile area.

I watched as Ross' deft fingers hurried to finish the operation before a sudden cloud of dust or a fly could contaminate his work. Flies landed on his face and walked back and forth across it throughout the procedure. Working with almost trance-like concentration, Ross gave no indication that he even noticed.

TWENTY-FIVE

For each of us, there were days when Sudan was a fantasyland. On those days, we fantasized about the things we couldn't do, couldn't see, couldn't eat, drink, touch, feel, hear or smell.

I imagined in greatest detail the taste and sound and sensation of biting into a crisp ice cold Red Delicious apple; the taste and smell of an enchilada; the sight and sound and smell of the waves from the Pacific Ocean crashing against the California coastline; the sound of a baseball meeting a bat and the smell of freshly mown grass at Candlestick Park in San Francisco.

One night I dreamed there would be a lot of mail the next day and most of it would be for me. The next day was my day off. I went to the post office and there was lots of mail, but none of it was for me.

Mike Schoenleber, a physician from Minneapolis, dreamed one night that Jane Fonda was at the foot of his bed. She was doing aerobic exercises and wasn't wearing much. Mike was shattered when he woke up. A few nights later, the other physician in Kassala at the time, Vic Snyder, dreamed he was on his way home. "I must be getting to be a short timer," he said later. "I dreamed I got mugged twice in the airport in New York."

Vic not only had fantasies like the rest of us, he helped fulfill then.

He'd sometimes give a fantasy sports broadcast as we drove out to camp in the morning. "The Cardinals won 6-5 last night," he'd report.

"I don't care about the Cardinals," I'd answer. "How did the Giants do?"

"They were playing the Cardinals."

"Oh."

Another morning, for the benefit of Terry Shields, a midwife from Philadelphia, he announced out of the blue: "The Cubs won a doubleheader yesterday from the Phillies. They've won seven straight now." In fact, none of us had the faintest idea how our favorite baseball teams were doing until we read about them in month-old newspaper clippings we'd occasionally receive, tucked in letters from home. It didn't matter whether we listened by short wave radio to English-language news on the BBC World Service, Voice of America, Radio Israel, Radio Moscow or Radio France, none ever gave a baseball score.

The one major fantasy most of us shared was for a bottle of ice-cold beer. Alcoholic beverages were forbidden in Sudan by sharia law, which was the law of the land in several fundamentalist Muslim countries. We viewed the beer ban with mixed feelings.

Few would dispute that alcohol can lead to aggressive and sometimes violent behavior. It was refreshing to walk the unlighted streets of Kassala at night without fear of being assaulted. Sudanese men seemed to be overwhelmingly passive, even though a good number of them considered a knife or long sharp sword part of their normal attire. You probably wouldn't want to meet one after dark if he'd just downed a six-pack of beer. On the other hand, what could possibly have tasted better than a cold beer on a 120-degree afternoon?

That's exactly what Vic thought. One afternoon, he came home with eight bottles of Eritrean beer that he had bought from a refugee for 50 pounds, or about $2 a bottle. He gave a bottle to each of us. We agreed unanimously it was worth the money, especially since it was his. I couldn't imagine anything providing more pleasure for $2. We decided then and there to get more beer, even though it would involve illicit dealings with a refugee smuggler and would cost us dearly. We settled on spending 100 pounds each, except for one person who wanted to buy only half the amount. We quickly got together a kitty of 850 pounds, about $300

As soon as we decided to buy more beer, a few people had second thoughts. It was a matter of conscience. Most of the refugees were unemployed and without income. The standard pay for those fortunate enough to have jobs was 140 pounds a month. That was one-sixth of the amount we had collected to spend on beer. Still, none of us felt we had to purposely live a life of self-denial in Sudan. We all wanted to enjoy the experience of being there. Was buying a dozen bottles of beer per person that excessive?

At the same time we were struggling with out consciences over the beer, the children's supplemental feeding program at Wad Sherife was facing cutbacks because of lack of funds. The 850 pounds would buy a lot of milk, high-energy biscuits, bananas and eggs for undernourished children. Marybeth's brother had given her $500 to help the refugees when she left the United States for Sudan. She had already given that to support the children's feeding program. I think Marybeth, Bob and a few others had also given some of their own money. The beer would taste good, though, no doubt about it. It seemed a small enough pleasure at a time and place where few pleasures were available.

Eventually, we did get the beer. Lynn Krueger had made contact with a source while working the night before in the cholera isolation hospital. It was amazing how high it lifted our spirits, since we were such a high-spirited group to begin with. We got 100 bottles of Meloti Beer that had been transported by camel, donkey and several middlemen from a brewery in Asmara, Eritrea. It had taken 12 days, using such primitive transportation, to get from Asmara to the *tukul* of a refugee at Wad Sherife. Finally, after a period of bartering, counting and recounting both money and bottles of beer, a deal was struck. Vic handed over 700 Sudanese pounds, about $230, in exchange for an old sugar sack containing 50 unlabeled bottles and a flimsy cardboard box containing 50 more.

Carefully, he and Lynn drove across the desert to Kassala with the beer. They were driving the jeep-style Toyota, the worst vehicle imaginable for transport of such precious cargo. This vehicle had a suspension system that could lift you off your seat at the apex of the smallest bump and seats that made you feel you'd dropped bottom-first onto a concrete floor when you came back down. Vic drove like he was carrying volatile explosives, creeping towards Kassala at barely 10 miles an hour.

Their caution was rewarded. When they arrived home just before dark, not a single bottle had been broken. All of us cheered wildly, ecstatic that our fantasy had been fulfilled.

Vaccines were moved temporarily from the freezing compartment to the lower section of the refrigerator to make room for the beer. No questions about priorities were asked. We put eight beers in the freezer, one for each of us, and another eight in the refrigerator itself. We didn't think we should open beers that had been so difficult to obtain while they were still at room temperature, over 100 degrees.

All through dinner and into the early evening, the same question was asked over and over: "Do you think they're cold enough yet?" We acted like kids in the back of a car, asking repeatedly: "Are we there yet?" Nobody noticed what time we opened the first bottles. Our usual bedtime was 9:00 o'clock, but we agreed it would be worthwhile to stay up until 10:00 or even 11:00 if necessary to drink a cold beer.

I had thought once before, after drinking a glass of fresh mango juice in the *souk,* that I had died and gone to heaven. The first swallow of beer that night was even better. We all felt similarly. The guilt of spending 100 pounds each for 14 beers, which was a slightly better price than we'd anticipated, disappeared with the first swallow. Rationalization was immediate. This is money going into the Eritrean economy, we told ourselves. Buying this beer is helping a lot of people. What are we here for, if not to help people? I felt very, very good about how I'd spent my 100 pounds.

We each downed our first beer fairly quickly, much as we tried to prolong it and savor each swallow. Each of us, that is, except for

Ross, the doctor from outer space. Ross poured his into a glass and swilled it down while some of the others were still uncapping theirs.

Someone moved the second round of beers from the refrigerator to the freezer when the first ones came out, but they never got a chance to get as cold as the first ones. When Vic checked the freezer, he reported that the beer was still warm but not too warm, "maybe you could even describe it as slightly cool," and asked if anybody wanted to have another one with him. We were forced to keep him company.

All it took was one swallow of warm beer to get Bob Enik in the mood to bring out his left-handed guitar and entertain us for the rest of the night. Bob was lead guitarist of a group in Massachusetts before coming to Sudan. He could play any song we could name. He knew songs by the hundreds.

Bob was still singing when someone thought he'd peek in the refrigerator, just in case something had been overlooked. There were two more cold ones. We divided them equally into five glasses, 0.4 of a beer each, making a running total for the night of 2.4 beers for the five of us still awake, two for Ross and one for Lynn.

We ended the night feeling very mellow, serene and satisfied as Bob sang John Lennon's "Imagine":
"Imagine all the people, living life in peace,
You may say I'm a dreamer; I'm not the only one…"

TWENTY-SIX

Dear Daddy,
    I love you very much. Did you help anyone yet?
What I mean is, is anybody better yet? I miss you very
much Daddy.
    Love, Rosanna

    (Excerpted from a letter, which came with hand-drawn
colored pictures of a rainbow, a Sudanese flag and a heart,
from my seven-year-old daughter)

Letters from home did more to boost morale than any bottle of
beer ever did, although they arrived in Kassala with about the same
predictability as Meloti Beer. Sometimes they came two or three
times a week, sometimes once every two weeks. One never knew in
advance.

    We all taught ourselves not to expect mail, as a defense against
disappointment. No one ever felt compelled to hide his or her joy
upon receiving a letter. It was always easy to spot those who had.
They were the ones walking around with huge grins on their faces.

    Some of the best times in Sudan were spent after coming home to the LARC house from Wad Sherife on an afternoon when everyone had received mail. We hurriedly made our tomato or canned cheese sandwiches, poured our glasses of cold orange or guava juice and then sat around the table in the back garden to read our letters. First, we read them silently to ourselves. Then, we read the highlights aloud to one another. Finally, we passed around photographs and newspaper clippings that had been enclosed with the letters. Sometimes, because we were so contented, more than an hour passed before anyone moved from his chair.

Our letters came from all over the world. Some came from places where no one even knew anybody. They must have come by all means of transport, to judge from the varying length of time they took to reach us. More than once, letters arrived with a notation on the envelope "Misdirected to Sweden."

The average letter spent two weeks in transit between a post office in the United States or Europe and the post office in Kassala. Once I received a letter than had come from California in just nine days. The very next day, I received another from the same person that had been mailed 50 days before.

Several friends at the hospital where I worked in California wrote to me one week. All their letters were mailed simultaneously in three identical air mail envelopes, numbered "1 of 3," "2 of 3" and "3 of 3." Two of them arrived the same day, the third 10 days later. Where had the other one gone during the interval, around the world in the opposite direction? Another time, after two weeks without a letter from my wife Margaret, I received four from her the same day. They had four different postmarks, spanning a period of 15 days.

The ultimate frustration was to receive an empty package. Bob and Marybeth got a parcel one day with more than $30 in U.S. postage stamps attached. There wasn't anything inside the package except empty space, just plain ordinary air.

Letters departing Sudan fared better than those coming in. I kept getting letters saying, in effect, that the one I had sent didn't take long at all to arrive. I sent letters only, not postcards, as one often does when in a foreign country. The only postcards available in Kassala, a city of 106,000, were produced in Egypt and didn't depict anything Sudanese. One pictured a swarthy-looking couple in western wedding clothes, cutting a wedding cake. Another showed a group of white kids sitting around a birthday cake. Judging from the haircuts and clothing, the latter photo looked like it was taken in about 1953.

Another rarity in Sudan was the 40-piaster postage stamp, which was odd since it cost 40 piasters to send a letter overseas. The post office in Kassala ran out of them in mid-May and a new supply still had not arrived three months later. We could affix any combination we liked of twos, eights and tens, so long as they totaled 40. It was rumored you could buy a 40-piaster stamp in Khartoum, the capital city, but the rumor was never confirmed.

It dawned on me one evening as I was writing a letter home that, as long as I had known my wife, more than 15 years, and my children, all their lives, none of us ever had written a letter to any of the others. We'd never before been apart for more than a few days.

Dear Rosanna,

Last time you wrote to me, you asked if anyone had gotten better yet. Well, I'll tell you: some get better, some don't. Some are just so starved and sick that they die, no matter what we do. Sometimes it is very sad, and the mothers and fathers and brothers and sisters are sad. But sometimes they are very strong and understanding, too.

One mother said the other day after her little girl died: "Everyone belongs to God." Then they took their little girl out and buried her under a mound of dirt, like hundreds before her, without any marker like in our cemeteries. I felt sad the other day when I went out and saw where they bury people.

But mostly we are seeing people get better. The starving children get eggs and bananas and grapefruit and hot cereal and milk every day, and they gain weight and get stronger and they feel happier. They love to play, just like kids at home, although there aren't any toys here.

Sometimes Bob comes into the feeding centers with a puppet, or with a soccer ball he bought. The kids also have sack races with old sugar sacks Bob brought them. They love it when he plays with them.

Lots of love, Daddy

TWENTY-SEVEN

Although I have traveled widely since I was 15 years old, I was totally naïve and unworldly in matters of African folk medicine before arriving in Sudan. I should have been reading more of the articles in *National Geographic* instead of just looking at the photos and reading the captions. I was flabbergasted by some of the things I would hear and see.

My biggest shock was to learn of the widespread practice of female circumcision or infibulation. I had never heard of it before. This is surgery to remove a girl's clitoris, labia minora and the inner walls of her labia majora, and then suture the two sides of her vulva together.

Millions of women have been circumcised in about two dozen countries that form a wide band across central Africa from the Atlantic Ocean in the west to the Red Sea and Indian Ocean in the east. It is so common in many countries that most people can't conceive of anything else. I never met an Eritrean who said he thought the practice was the least bit unusual, and certainly not barbaric. Of course, I didn't raise the subject with everyone I met and I never discussed it with an Eritrean woman.

The historical origins are unknown. Anthropologists think it may be an ancient African puberty rite. One thing is certain. Its origins are not religious, although many women now believe it is a religious duty to be circumcised. Infibulation predates Islam, the primary religion in many of the countries where it is practiced. Muslims, Catholics, Protestants, Copts, aminists and non-believers all adhere to the tradition.

Many girls and women accept it as both a rite of womanhood and a woman's right. Although prohibited by law in some countries, including Sudan, the practice continues. It is said that any girl not circumcised feels she has been cheated of one of the important events of her life. Girls are lavished with gifts and attention before being circumcised. They are congratulated afterwards.

Both men and women see circumcision as necessary for the preservation of the reputations and virginity of unmarried women. The belief holds that an uncircumcised woman is somehow impure and as such will have difficulty finding a husband. Even some Africans who have been educated on other continents, who can see no other benefits of infibulation, justify it so not to deny their daughters the chance to marry.

Typically, an old woman using an unsterile knife or razor blade performs the circumcision. Several women hold down the girl, who is usually seven or eight years old, during the procedure. Infections and other post-infibulation complications are common. A woman's wedding night and the first weeks of marriage are not always remembered as times of great joy and pleasure. During childbirth, infibulated women must be opened surgically to allow passage of their babies. Afterwards, they are sewn up again.

It is difficult as a non-African to be non-judgmental about the practice of female circumcision. The American practice of male circumcision for no particular reason must seem equally strange to most of the world. Less than a quarter of the world's men are circumcised. The overwhelming majority of circumcised men are Muslims and Jews, who have it done as religious rituals. The United States is the only country in the world where non-religious circumcision is commonly done.

I found most other African folk treatments and cures easier to equate to orthodox western ways than I did female circumcision.

During the first week after childbirth, Eritrean women often spent hours squatting in their *tukuls*, directly over small pits filled with red-hot coals. The rising heat was beneficial to healing. Susan Smith, the LARC medical director, said she had observed a similar practice in Thailand. American women sometimes use electric episiotomy lamps for the same purpose as they lay in their hospital beds after childbirth.

Eritreans have their uvulas removed shortly after birth. The uvula is a small fleshy appendage that hangs from the center of the back of the roof of the mouth. Everybody is born with one but I've never met anyone who knows what function it serves. My students at Wad Sherife grew up believing a human being can't swallow if his uvula isn't removed. Few had ever seen an adult with his uvula intact until they met me. I never had seen anyone who didn't have one until I met them. They thought it was interesting that I had had my tonsils removed as a child, at a time when their function was unclear and American doctors almost routinely recommended their removal.

We saw the results of one fairly abhorrent folk remedy almost every day at Wad Sherife: bodies covered by patterns of small round scars, the size of the heads of nails. Indeed, red-hot nails had been applied to draw pain out of these people's bodies, much as Americans or Europeans would use hot water bottles, heating pads or a hot soaks.

Observation of the scars was a useful diagnostic tool for us. If a person had dozens of scars that appeared to be of varying ages over his chest, for example, we knew he had a chronic lung condition. This was often a good lead towards a diagnosis of tuberculosis.

An alternative heat treatment was to burn crumpled paper in a small glass or cup and then place the open end of the cup firmly against the area in pain. The fire burned off the oxygen, creating a vacuum in the cup or glass, which in turn caused a suction effect, drawing out the pain. It also left blisters equal to the circumference of the cup. One day, one of my students and I saw a teenaged boy with two perfectly round, two-inch wide blisters on his neck and upper chest. We looked in the back of his mouth with a flashlight and found he had tonsillitis.

TWENTY-EIGHT

If Ross Tannebaum and I remember only one thing about each other 25 years after we've left Sudan, it probably will be that we spent the worst days of our lives together. We came to that conclusion on the way home from our five-day vacation on the Red Sea coast.

Almost everyone from every relief agency in eastern Sudan wanted to take a vacation on the Red Sea. The allure of a large body of water after spending two months in the middle of a parched desert was irresistible. Besides, there wasn't any place else to go. The only other spot on the map even worth considering for a few days rest and recreation was Khartoum. Everybody had already been there once, on the way into the country, and few wanted to go a second time until they were passing through on the way back out. There was also Kassala, which some people and one guidebook called The Paris of Eastern Sudan, but we were already there.

You had to spend most of the first and last days of your holiday on a bus, whether you chose to go to Khartoum or Port Sudan on the Red Sea coast. Ross and I decided that since we had to do this, we would ride in style. We bought tickets on a semi-modern looking bus that had AIR CONDITION painted on the side. It was air conditioned, all right. Any time you opened or closed your window, you changed the condition of the air, from still to moving or vice-versa. The bus was a rolling sweatbox by 6:30 a.m. and it only got hotter as the day went along.

For three hours, we traveled non-stop over the best part of the only paved road in Sudan, across country that looked like the moon with a few goats, thorn trees and a scattering of blown out truck tires. Then, still not halfway to Port Sudan, we stopped for breakfast at a roadside truck stop café in a large *recubba* that looked a lot like a Wad Sherife feeding center.

We ate a breakfast of grilled goat meat and bread, washed down with a sickly sweet soft drink called Alkola. The goat smelled wonderful as it was being cooked over a charcoal fire. It didn't taste bad either. However, it was so tough that you had to swallow each piece whole. No amount of chewing would break it down. It was like charcoal-broiled goat-flavored gum. The bread was superb, as most everywhere I went in Sudan. It was at once coarse, grainy and chewy and it cost about three cents. My only complaint was there was a small stick in the middle of the bread. A week before, I got a raisin-sized stone in my bread.

We arrived in Port Sudan in mid-afternoon and found a room at the Olympic Park Hotel for about $3.00 per person per night. I immediately went for a shower down the hall from our room. I took off my clothes and placed my soap and shampoo in the soap dish that inexplicably was attached to the wall above the door, at a height I barely could reach. I turned on the shower but no water came out. I dressed again, retrieved my soap and shampoo from above the door and found another shower across the hall. This one had running water.

Ross and I walked around town for a while and began to wonder if we had gotten off the bus in the wrong place. Could this really be Port Sudan, the only seaport in the largest country in Africa? There were buildings, but they all looked unoccupied. Port Sudan looked like a ghost town, some British colonial outpost last inhabited in about 1950.

We found the Red Sea Club ("Members Only") on the waterfront, where we took out memberships for less than $1.00 each. We were confident we would meet someone there who could direct us to the best restaurants, nightlife and snorkeling areas in and around Port Sudan.

We met an Indonesian seaman who said there was some great nightlife just down the road.

"How far?" Ross asked.

"Three days," he said. "Sailors like Port Sudan because they can save their money. There is nothing to spend it on."

We met a relief worker from Oxfam, the British development agency, and asked him if there were any good restaurants in Port Sudan. "No," he answered, saying all there was to say on the subject.

Two Romanian sailors asked what we were doing in Sudan. We told them we worked with refugees. They wanted to know if we were earning a lot of money. We told them no, none at all. "Excuse me for laughing," said one of them, "but that is not normal." The other added: "The worst thing that could happen to a person would be to be stuck here. I would hang myself."

It was so hot that night that Ross took the thin mattress off his bed and went up on the roof of the hotel to sleep. I sat for a while under the slowly rotating overhead fan in our room, trying to write a letter and thinking it must be at least 130 degrees. Sweat kept running off my face and dripping onto my letter, even though it was 10:00 o'clock at night. Finally, I dragged my mattress up to the roof, too.

We were awakened early the next morning, long before sunrise, not by flies, as was our usual custom, but by crows. In the early light of dawn, about 30 large, black, raucous-sounding birds demanded loudly and persistently that we arise and vacate their territory. I was quite happy to do so, even though it was only 5:15 a.m., because I woke up feeling I either had to shit or fart. I didn't want to make any assumptions about which and possibly be wrong.

One learns to truly appreciate a good fart when traveling in an underdeveloped country. You learn quickly not to trust the feeling of an impending one. As often as not, the feeling means another bout of explosive diarrhea is eminent. No vacation could be complete without this, I thought.

Meanwhile, Ross had developed a bad cold and laryngitis. By 6:50 a.m., after walking through the *souk* to find some fresh fruit for breakfast, we were already consciously searching for shade. I asked Ross if he thought Port Sudan was the hottest place on earth. He could only nod affirmatively. His voice was completely gone.

The real point of our vacation was not to spend time in Port Sudan, but to go snorkeling at Arous, a resort 30 miles up the Red Sea coast. Since Ross had been struck speechless, I went alone to the tourist office to make arrangements. How much will it cost to stay two nights, I wanted to know.

"300 pounds."

Now I was momentarily speechless. A normal monthly wage in Sudan is 140 pounds, about $45.

"But we can do it for 200 pounds," the man in the tourist office said, sensing he might end up with nothing if he set the price too high. "100 pounds, full board. Do you have a car?"

Fortunately, we didn't, because it wouldn't have occurred to me to ask if they had a road, which they didn't.

"Okay, if you go today, we will take you. Transportation is free."

Free transportation out of Port Sudan, today, to anywhere, sounded like the answer to a prayer. We returned to our hotel, gathered our belongings in our backpacks and were on our way within the hour.

TWENTY-NINE

The ride from Port Sudan to Arous, in the cab of a battered gray Land Rover, was mind-bending, to borrow an old phrase from the sixties. We assumed that since both Port Sudan and Arous were on the Red Sea coast, and since there was absolutely nothing in between, not even a road, we would simply drive along the coast until reaching our destination.

Instead, we drove for an hour and a half without seeing anything that gave the faintest hint we were within a thousand miles of a drop of water. This was the most hostile looking desert I had seen yet. If the driver had dropped us off half way, we'd have been dead before dark, like dried apricots.

It was so hot that I saw a mirage in every direction I looked. I saw something green on the horizon ahead, but it was floating. I saw something blue on the right, where the Red Sea was supposed to be, but it also was floating, just above the horizon. The surface of the earth looked like it was breaking up. My mind knew my eyes were deceiving me, but hard as I looked, I still saw vast areas of blue and green, floating just above the ground.

The whole area looked as if it had once been a nuclear test site, scorched, sterilized and unable to support any life form for another

20,000 years. I wondered if God had intentionally created the land this way, or we had discovered an oversight in His grand plan for the world. Did American astronauts land on some lunar Sudan and only think there was no life on the moon? Did they ever leave earth, or was the whole thing a hoax, with the landing and moonwalk filmed in this remote part of eastern Sudan? If someone was to come to this spot from another planet, he could easily think that earth was uninhabitable, turn around and go home without knowing any better.

Suddenly, we went over a little rise in the desert, and off to the right we could see the blue waters of the Red Sea and a row of about 15 little bungalows paralleling the shore. This was Arous. It looked like an advertisement for Club Med, except there were no volleyball nets, no girls in bikinis on the beach. In fact, there wasn't anybody there except a family that lived and worked there.

Ross and I were shown to a bungalow. There were light fixtures and air-conditioning units but no apparent source of electricity. We hoped there was a generator that would be activated later. There was a washbasin, shower and toilet but no water. When we complained, they moved us to another bungalow with running water. It remained to be seen whether there would be electricity.

I lay down to take a short nap but it was so hot and I was sweating so profusely, my ears kept filling with water. When I gave up the idea of a nap and stood up, the mattress was soaking wet. I decided to take a shower to cool off before lunch. The water came out of the shower so hot I nearly scalded myself. I wouldn't take a shower that hot in the middle of winter at home. This was unheated water. There were no separate handles for hot and cold.

The cook, a refugee from Eritrea, must have thought Ross and I were a pair of white gluttons. For lunch, he served us a huge platter of spaghetti, two pitchers of water and bread. It was all we could comfortably eat. Then he brought out a platter of meat, mashed potatoes and peas. That was followed by cantaloupe and coffee. It was embarrassing to be served so much food in such a poor country, by a refugee from an even poorer country where people were dying of starvation.

We wondered where the peas came from. We didn't like to think too much about the meat because we had seen the meat market in the *souk* in Port Sudan that morning. I had been so impressed by the concentration of flies on one particular camel's head that I took a close-up photo of it.

There was a freezer behind the bar in the dining area, beneath a long price list of wines, beers and mixed drinks. This was a reminder of days long past in Sudan. None of the drinks was available now, of course, since alcoholic beverages were illegal under present-day law. The freezer was used for storing bottles of water and Alkola. It was kept locked at all times. We wondered why, but didn't ask. Since there was no electricity and the generator ran only two hours each night, the water in the freezer was not much cooler than the shower water.

We also wondered where the good snorkeling was. We couldn't ask because Ross and I were the only ones in Arous who spoke English. After our initial venture into the water, we wondered if we had mistakenly come to the Dead Sea, not the Red Sea. The water was so murky we could barely see the bottom, even though it was only knee deep. If there wasn't something dead in the water, it sure smelled like it.

***

Can paradise and hell be so close together that one actually touches the other, that one begins where the other ends, with nothing in between?

The heat in Arous created an absolute hell. This was Hot with a capital H, hot like when you stand too close to a campfire and are afraid for a brief instant that your pants have caught fire. I told Ross that if I had $1,000, I'd give it to him to fan me for 30 minutes, to cool me down enough so I could fall asleep and be out of my misery. It was so hot that the sky, without a cloud to be seen in any direction, wasn't even blue. It was a bright pale gray, like steam. I felt no cooler when we waded into the sea, 100, 200, 300 yards from shore. We were still only up to our waists in tepid water.

Then we reached the edge of the reef, put on our masks and lay face down in the water. Suddenly, we were in paradise. We were a million miles from hell. I entered a world I never knew existed. We were surrounded by thousands of tropical fish, in splendid pastel pinks and greens, in neon blues, in comical shapes—round ones with needle noses, ones that looked like legless zebras with yellow heads.

The heat of Sudan seemed like something from another lifetime, yet we had experienced it only seconds before. Could it possibly have been that bad? I quickly lost count of the times I saw the most beautiful fish I'd ever seen, only to see another one that I thought was even more beautiful. Just as it is impossible to make someone understand how hot it was in Arous, it is equally impossible to convey how beautiful the undersea world there was.

Even paradise has its flaws, though. There was agony with the ecstasy. Even though we were never in water that was more than waist deep and there was no surf, I felt nervous, maybe even a little scared. I must have been swept away by the sea and drowned or killed by a shark in a previous life. Though totally absorbed by the beauty of the tropical fish, I periodically found myself wishing I was wearing my glasses and had a rearview mirror so I could see if anything was coming up from behind to attack me. Several times, I stood up and reoriented myself as a reassurance that I hadn't been swept out to sea.

Later in the day, we met an old fisherman on the beach. He probably knew better than anyone if there was anything dangerous in the water at Arous. It didn't occur to me to ask him, and our conversation was pretty much limited to sign language anyway, since we didn't speak each other's languages.

For dinner that night, we had peanut soup, French fried potatoes and a fish the old man had caught in his net less than an hour before. It was one of the best meals I ate in Sudan. At lunch the next day, we were served a salad and then told there wouldn't be anything more to eat. They said they didn't have a match to light the stove to cook the lunch. Brilliant! We were at a resort, advertised on travel posters that were sent to travel agents around the world by the Sudanese government, and they couldn't serve lunch because nobody had a match.

Luckily, there was one creative thinker amongst us. He searched the bungalows, one by one, until he found a single wooden match under a bed. He brought the match to the kitchen. With everyone gathered around, he turned on the gas, struck the match and lit the stove. We had a late lunch of fried fish and chips and continued to have regular cooked meals until our departure.

We saw the old fisherman again, only minutes before we left Arous to go back to Port Sudan. He motioned to us to follow him along the beach. He seemed to want to show us something. We followed him for about 100 yards, finally arriving at a large rock on which he was drying the remains of a five-foot-long shark. He gestured to us that he'd caught it the day before, on the edge of the reef where Ross and I had done most of our snorkeling.

THIRTY

We found out exactly how hot it was when we got back to Port Sudan. We visited an American ship that was unloading grain for the relief effort. While on board, we talked for a long time in the air-conditioned crew's mess with the first mate and the bosun. The first mate had lived and worked at sea for 15 years. He had been to virtually every port city in the world outside of those in Australia and New Zealand. He said that Port Sudan was the clear-cut absolute worst place he'd ever been. It was comforting to find someone who shared our feelings.

The bosun, during his many years at sea, had developed the habit of measuring the air temperature on the shady side of the ship at 1:00 o'clock every afternoon, wherever he was in the world. He kept a record of his findings in a logbook.

"How hot is it here today?" one of us asked.

"118 in the shade," he reported. "Probably six to eight degrees warmer in the sun." Now we knew it was officially hot, not just in our minds.

I hoped I would never forget how it felt to be so hot. I wanted to remember the heat, exactly how it made me feel, so I would never again be tempted to go anywhere in the world as hot as this. Not for any reason. Ever. There's a story I'll always cling to as a reminder. I met a Canadian who told me he left a brand new candle in his window of his room one morning when he left for work near the Lalmba refugee camp at Wad el Hileu. When he came home that afternoon, there was a puddle of wax and a piece of unburned string on the windowsill.

More significantly, we found out firsthand why the food being sent from all over the world was taking so long to reach the refugee camps. Port Sudan was a bottleneck. It became painfully obvious as soon as we saw the port facilities. Sudan covers an area the size of the eastern third of the United States and at the time had a population of 18 million. Its one seaport with berths for 18 ships had for a long time been adequate to serve its needs. However, the facilities for unloading the ships were shockingly primitive and inadequate for present needs. The demands placed on both facilities and manpower by the incoming famine relief supplies brought the whole system to its knees.

The American ship we visited was a huge oil tanker, several hundred feet long. Its tanks had been steam-cleaned, dried and loaded with more than a hundred tons of sorghum. The ship had an on-board system to pump the loose grain from the tanks and deposit it into a silo on the dock.

Once there, though, the grain had to be put into hand-held bags with a capacity of 100 pounds each. The bags had to be stitched closed and loaded by hand, one by one, onto trucks. Barefoot undernourished-looking stevedores, working under the blazing sun from dawn to dusk, did all the lifting. It took two men to hoist each bag onto the shoulders of another who carried it. Some of the stevedores appeared to weigh no more than the bags they carried.

We were told that ships lay anchored off shore for as long as two weeks, waiting for a berth to become vacant, before they could unload their emergency food supplies.

Another problem: there weren't enough trucks in the whole of Sudan to move the grain out as quickly as it was bagged and loaded. Most trucks were needed to satisfy the normal supply demands of the

Sudanese people. Those that transported emergency food supplies carried unbelievably large loads and suffered frequent breakdowns as a result of overloading. They had to travel regularly to remote supply depots in villages or refugee camps that were located miles from the paved two-lane road connecting Port Sudan to major inland towns. The trucks took a terrible beating from the heat, dust and rough surfaces as soon as they left the road. After the rains began, they sometimes became mired in axle-deep mud.

Bob Geldof, the Irish rock star responsible for the spectacularly successful Band Aid and Live Aid fund-raising projects, was one of the first to recognize this problem. His response was to donate somewhere in the neighborhood of 90 trucks to Sudan, in addition to the more publicized food and medical supplies.

Much to our surprise and chagrin, Ross and I rode most of the way home to Kassala, standing in the back of a truck. We arrived at the bus loading area in Port Sudan at 5:45 a.m. and were told that the bus on which we had reserved seats was "out of order." Our money was refunded and we were told to find another bus. Fortunately, we were able to do so. We were underway by 6:15. Unfortunately, that bus soon was out of order, too.

At 11:00 o'clock, with the sun climbing toward its apex and the bus in no-man's land several hours from both Port Sudan and Kassala, it broke down. The driver tinkered around under the hood for a while, trying unsuccessfully to find and repair the problem. Eventually, another bus stopped just in front of us to change a tire. When that had been done, our driver got onto that bus and disappeared with it down the road and over the horizon. He had said nothing about when he might return.

A few passengers got off our bus and hitched rides on passing trucks. There were no cars. Later, several men got off our bus and flagged down an empty truck headed for Port Sudan. After half an hour of bargaining over a price, 26 of us paid 10 pounds each (about $3.00) to the driver, who agreed to reverse his direction and take us all to Kassala. Most everyone was savvy enough to be carrying a water bottle, which was fortunate, because we spent four and a half hours in the direct sun before we reached Kassala.

In retrospect, Ross and I decided standing in the back of a truck all afternoon was probably no less uncomfortable than sitting in a bus. Being so exposed to the open air while traveling 50 miles an hour, we were cooled by the wind. The temperature by late afternoon, figuring in the wind chill factor, was probably less than 100 degrees.

THIRTY-ONE

One Sunday, about two weeks after Ross and I returned from the Red Sea, most of us in our house in Kassala decided to take our weekly day off together. We had spent nearly every day of the past two months together already, but this was to be a special day, one we wanted to spend totally indulged in one another's company. It would be our last day together as a group.

Vic Snyder was leaving the next morning to return to the United States. Many of the rest of us would be going our separate ways during the next two weeks. We had become so close during our time together that no one wanted to see anyone else leave. We particularly didn't want Vic to go. We had moments of real melancholy as we tried to imagine life in Sudan without his humor. He was funnier than all the rest of us put together.

We decided to spend our last day climbing the *Jebels*, a small but breathtakingly spectacular range of mountains between Kassala and Wad Sherife. There was something mystical about the *Jebels*. They were not mountains as one normally thinks of mountains, with foothills and increasingly steep ascents leading to high peaks. The *Jebels* were giant monoliths that arose almost perpendicularly from the monotonously flat desert. They were like islands in the desert. If the desert had been blue, it would have been easy to imagine the *Jebels* as Bora Bora or some equally exotic place in the South Pacific.

Unlike the pyramids in Egypt, one could not even begin to speculate about how the *Jebels* got there. It was difficult to believe they simply erupted from the desert floor one day, or were left there after millions of years of erosion, because they arose so sharply and to such a great height. At the same time, it was even more difficult to believe something so massive was dropped or had been flung to earth from outer space.

We drove past the *Jebels* on the way to and from Wad Sherife every day, twice a day. I never once failed to be moved by their beauty and mystique. The entire range could be circled in a four-wheel drive vehicle in an hour during dry weather, although not at all after the arrival of the first rain.

Phena Cullen and I walked around the backside of the *Jebels* one day after the rains had come. We nearly met with disaster when I stepped into quicksand and was down to my knees before I realized what had happened. I don't know if I could have gotten out if I had been alone.

Three species of large birds and mammals lived on the *Jebels.* Vultures, with four-to-five foot wingspans, nested on the most remote ledges of the most precarious cliffs. Mountain goats roamed rock faces that from afar looked almost vertical. Fairly regularly, we drove to within 50 yards of a family of baboons that came down to rummage through the garbage dump at the foot of the *Jebels* on the outskirts of Kassala. The baboons were fierce-looking creatures with doglike faces and short tails. They walked right onto the heap of smoldering garbage in search of food. This sometimes created a surrealistic scene: baboons, partially surrounded by rising smoke, looking as if they were having a baboon barbecue.

Inexperienced amateurs could climb many of the lesser peaks of the *Jebels*, without need of any special equipment. No man had ever conquered the most difficult peak, according to a local guidebook.

We all got up at 5:00 o'clock on the morning of our last day together. It was important to begin climbing early and get back by midday because of the heat. There was an eerie sort of peace about the morning. We had been planning our assault on the *Jebels* all week long, but on the morning of the climb, three people suddenly dropped out.

Ross felt that several patients in the hospital at Wad Sherife were too ill to be left all morning without a physician's attention. He decided to go to work as usual. Bob had a bad cold and the general Sudanese malaise, probably a viral infection that affected all of us from time to time. He spent the morning alone in a room, writing a blues song. I couldn't go climbing because the two doctors, Vic and Ross, wouldn't let me.

I had an infection in my left leg that had progressed from a barely visible scratch one week to a small but bothersome sore the next. To treat it, I was taking antibiotic capsules four times a day, covering the wound with gauze dressings, and elevating the leg while applying hot compresses to improve circulation. This had seemed to me an overly aggressive treatment of a scratch.

The infection turned into full-blown cellulitis a few days before we were to climb the *Jebels*. My lower leg became red, hot, painful and swollen from ankle to knee. Clear colorless fluid oozed from the wound, which had grown to the size of 25-cent piece. The swelling completely obliterated the ankle on the outside of my leg.

By the morning we were supposed to climb the *Jebels*, Vic and Ross had become seriously concerned about my leg, even if I still had not. Vic said if the infection didn't respond to a second antibiotic I had begun taking, I might have to be flown from Sudan to a country where I could be hospitalized and treated with intravenous antibiotics. I was sure he was joking until both he and Ross insisted I stay behind, keep my leg elevated, and read "the short story," as they called it, instead of climbing the *Jebels*. They had been encouraging me to read "the short story" for several days.

The story was *The Snows of Kilimanjaro*, one part of a collection of stories by Ernest Hemingway. I could remember a time in my teens or early twenties when reading Hemingway was fashionable. I read a few of his novels and several of his stories. I thought he was a great writer. Then, some critic pointed out something that soured me on him. Hemingway made his career of glorifying drunkenness, fist fighting, bull fighting, hunting, lying, and viewing women as mere sexual prey. I'd never forgotten that assessment.

Nevertheless, I agreed to read "the short story" that morning. Ross loaned me the book before leaving for Wad Sherife. After everyone else had left for the *Jebels*, I climbed in under Marybeth's mosquito net to protect myself from flies, propped my leg up on three pillows, lay back and began to read.

The Snows of Kilimanjaro is the story of a man in Africa on safari, dying from gangrene in his leg, which came as a result of a small and harmless-looking scratch. The story is of his last hours, awaiting the arrival of a plane that is to evacuate him to a place where he can receive more aggressive treatment that may or may not save his life. He never finds out which. He dies before the plane gets there.

THIRTY-TWO

Except for the baboons and goats on the *Jebels*, we rarely encountered any of the exotic wildlife one associates with Africa. There were camels by the hundreds, but all were either domesticated work animals or in controlled herds to be bred, sold or traded. Many eventually would be slaughtered for their meat. I didn't see a single snake in six months. I saw only a few camel spiders, which were huge nocturnal creatures that looked like anemic tarantulas. Mike Schoenleber had a better description; he said they looked like "crabs with hair." Indeed, they could be a good six inches across.

The only things that scared me were dogs. Wild dogs, frankly, scared the shit out of me. I had a fear of dogs that went back to 1966 or 1967, when I was surrounded and within minutes of being savaged by a pack of wild dogs in the mountains of Lebanon. One had already sunk his teeth into my right leg when I was rescued. The fear I felt that day scarred my psyche. I had nightmares for years.

When I came to Kassala, I learned quickly never to go for my morning run without carrying a good throwing rock in each hand to ward off the dogs that roamed the banks of the River Gash. Most had been trained, and at first sight of a rock sailing through the air in their direction, put their tails between their legs and ran off in the opposite direction. Many would slink away as soon as I cocked my arm or bent over to pick up a rock.

Kassala was full of dogs, but fortunately, its dirt streets were littered with stones. I thought there was nothing to fear but a sneak attack. I found out otherwise one night when a group of us were driving home from a movie. We rounded a corner not 100 yards from the theater and met a pack of about 30 wild dogs. Chills ran down my spine. Recollections of Lebanon flashed through my mind. I could have walked around that corner, I thought to myself. Alone.

David Schmidt must have had similar feelings about dogs as I, or similar fears, or maybe we just shared the same perverse sense of humor. We agreed it would be great fun to drive full speed through the middle of the pack to see how many dogs we could kill. Luckily for the dogs, there were others in the pickup truck whose better judgment prevailed.

My nervousness only increased a month or so later when I left Kassala and was reassigned to work at a Lalmba refugee settlement in Wad el Hileu. As I approached Wad el Hileu the first time, riding in the back of a pickup truck, we passed dozens of large dogs, some in packs. I noticed very few rocks along the dirt track across the desert. I wondered if I should have brought my own. I didn't want to give up my early morning runs. They were a simple yet important part of my life. At the same time, I didn't want to risk being bitten. I had already heard rumors of an American Peace Corps volunteer in Africa who had died after a rabid kitten had licked an open sore on her hand.

On closer inspection of the landscape during my first week in Wad el Hileu, I discovered there were rocks scattered about, although so few that I feared I might not find one when I needed it. I decided I'd gather a collection as I found them, save them and take a few with me each morning when I set out on my run. Any I didn't need, I could keep for another day. And so, I accumulated and maintained a small collection of flat, smooth, round or oval-shaped stones, each approximately three inches in diameter, on the windowsill above the head of my bed.

I became very judicious about how I spent them. Sometimes I'd fire off a warning shot for educational purposes. I threw intending to actually hit a dog only a few times. I could never figure out why there were so many dogs in a place so desolate and poor as Wad el Hileu. They didn't appear to be anybody's pets, working dogs or watch dogs. I don't know who fed them. Sometimes their barking and howling were the only sounds of an otherwise silent night. Occasionally, the sounds became frenzied, as if all the members of the pack had turned against one outsider, or against another member of the pack.

My early morning runs took me from the edge of the refugee settlement, where we lived, past a defecation site, and along a dirt track across an expanse of grass and scrub and fields of dura. I had wondered for months how the refugees wiped and cleaned themselves after squatting in the defecation fields at both Wad Sherife and Wad el Hileu. They didn't use toilet paper. There was very little grass. They rarely appeared to be carrying containers of water. And then one morning, while passing the defecation site, I found out. They wiped themselves with small, flat, smooth stones— the ones I'd been picking up at every opportunity, stacking in my windowsill, and carrying in each hand every morning when I went out to run.

THIRTY-THREE

I never did get to climb the *Jebels*, but I did make a surreptitious visit to Eritrea. I had become so close to so many of the Eritreans I met at Wad Sherife, I wanted desperately to see their homeland, to see the country they had been forced to leave. Whether they had left because of famine or because of the war, each had left against his will. Every single one wanted to go back some day. How could I live and work every day for months among people who so loved their country, within sight of its border, and not want to go there myself?

I had been trying almost since my first week in Kassala to arrange a trip. I had asked dozens of individuals how I could manage to get in. I had made contact with representatives of the Eritrean Liberation Front (ELF) and the Eritrean People's Liberation Front (EPLF), both of which had offices in Kassala. I think both groups genuinely wanted to escort me to sites in Eritrea they thought would make the right political impressions, in case there was uncertainty about which side I was most sympathetic to in the civil war. At the same time, they were concerned about my safety. I was repeatedly given the same answer when I asked if they had managed to arrange a visit: "We'd love to take you, but with the rainy season, and with the bombing so close, it's too dangerous..."

Nevertheless, I still wanted to cross the border, even if only to the first village, even if only for an hour or two. There would be something symbolic about going. It would show my Eritrean friends that I truly cared about their country when I spoke of wanting to go, that my words were not empty ones. I was also curious.

One afternoon, on the way home from Wad Sherife, a vehicle pulled along side the one in which I was riding. Mary Bowe, the Irish nurse, was in the other vehicle, waving furiously at us to stop. Both vehicles stopped and Mary called out the window: "Do you want to go to Eritrea, Richard? We're going there now." I didn't need to be asked twice.

Mary and Phena Cullen were riding in one of the two jeep-style Mitsubishis belonging to the Swiss Disaster Relief Team. Also in the vehicles were four Swiss doctors and nurses, a Sudanese doctor and Tekle, a 17-year-old Eritrean who was one of the home visitors on the LARC medical team at Wad Sherife. One of the Swiss said they were all going across the border "just to take a look...if we can get in." None of us was carrying a passport.

We drove at 110 kilometers an hour, more than 65 mph, across the desert parallel to a line of steel telephone poles that probably had been installed more than half a century earlier by the Italians. At this point in time, they no longer had wires attached to them.

In the distance, reflecting yellow against the late afternoon sun, was a small square building that the Sudanese doctor said was the Sudanese border guards' post. He suggested we put our cameras out of sight before we got there. We stopped for a few minutes at the frontier while he got out and spoke briefly with the guards, two old men in green khaki uniforms. Then he got back in the car and we drove off, no questions asked, no passports required, out of Sudan and into Eritrea.

It seemed almost too easy. There wasn't any road leading to the border. There wasn't any fence along the border. There wasn't any border patrol of the Eritrean side. We easily could have avoided the border station on the Sudanese side if we had chosen to, by taking a less direct route. Or, we could have simply driven past the border guards without stopping.

I was disappointed to find the desert on the Eritrean side of the border looked no different than the desert on the Sudanese side. I mentioned that to one of the Swiss nurses, who agreed. The words had barely passed our lips when we began to notice subtle changes. There were a few more trees on the Eritrean desert. The bushes were marginally larger. Also, we were within a mile of the mountains that we had only seen silhouetted against the horizon from Wad Sherife.

We came to a deserted cluster of round houses with thatched grass roofs, no different than those on the Sudanese side of the border. We stopped and got out to take a few photos. We quickly realized they weren't deserted. People emerged from the houses, walking in twos and threes towards us. A total of 30 or 40 men, women and children came forward.

We communicated as best we could at the most basic level with lots of smiles, simple greetings in Arabic, handshakes and picture taking. They told the Sudanese doctor there was no food in their tiny village. They were aware of a refugee camp not far across the border, but they were unwilling to leave Eritrea. They were the last holdouts.

The doctor told them he would arrange for the Saudi Arabian Red Crescent to deliver food to the border the next day. The Saudi Red Crescent was the exception to the unwritten rule that all relief agencies cooperate and work together in Sudan. They did everything on their own, independent of everyone else. There was ample evidence that they were providing important services and doing a lot of good in their own way. The Sudanese doctor was the only person I'd met, though, who actually made any contact with them.

As we got back into our two vehicles, a touching thing unexpectedly happened. All the Eritreans burst into applause and stood clapping as we drove off towards the mountains. I wondered why.

When we reached the base of the mountains, we discovered the burial site of about a dozen Italians soldiers, killed in World War II. The Sudanese doctor and Tekle, the Eritrean teenager who had come with us, warned that it would be dangerous to wander much further from the border. We had covered only about a mile of countryside and had spent no more than an hour in Eritrea. Still, I felt pleasantly satisfied as we headed back towards the little yellow building with the two aging border guards, and across the Sudanese desert toward Kassala. It was only a postcard-sized memory, but an important one.

THIRTY-FOUR

My last days at Wad Sherife and in Kassala were emotional ones. There were overlapping moments of reflection and introspection, happiness and joy and then melancholy. There was a curious mixture of both great hope and despair for the future. I thought a lot about who and what I would miss the most, and also about some of the things I wouldn't miss at all. I reflected on my expectations and how they had turned out.

I also tried to keep an open mind about the next three months, which I'd be spending in another part of eastern Sudan with another group of *khawajas* from another relief agency working with another group of refugees.

From the day I found out I was coming to Sudan, I had looked forward to the experience of being one of very few white people in a totally black country. Most black people in North America and Europe have experienced being the only black in a large crowd of whites at one time or another. I had never experienced the reverse of that. I was curious to know how it would feel. I don't know what I expected to feel, but I was a little disappointed when, after three months, I didn't feel anything at all.

I was constantly aware of being a foreigner because I couldn't speak Arabic, but I would have felt no less foreign in France or China or Finland. Strangers continually addressed us as *khawaja*, which translated to foreigner. Almost without exception, *khawaja!* was offered as a cheerful and enthusiastic greeting. Even when said in a slightly accusative tone, it never seemed like a racial slur.

Everyone in Sudan seemed color blind. I became color blind myself. After the first few weeks were behind me, I don't recall ever looking around and thinking: "hey, everybody here's black but me." It only occasionally occurred to me that I was white.

Among the things I expected to miss most about Wad Sherife were my daily visits with children in the feeding center and hospital. Both were within 50 yards of my classroom. The children there were at once the most pathetic children in the camp and the ones who gave us the most pleasure and satisfaction. They made us aware that no matter how bad our hardships and discomforts, it had been worthwhile to have come here.

These were the children the world saw on television. Some appeared to be no more than tiny black skin-covered skeletons with sunken eyes, barely strong enough to sit upright unassisted, often too tired and weak to brush away the flies around their eyes and mouths.

The worst of these children, in terms of their malnourishment, weighed less than 70 percent of normal for their height and had upper arm circumferences of less than five inches, about the size of a carrot. These children stayed all day long in the feeding center in what was called the therapeutic feeding program. They were fed milk, eggs, high-energy biscuits, bananas, grapefruit and hot cereal made from corn and soy meal. They also received a multi-vitamin tablet every morning, were screened daily for eye and ear infections and other obvious treatable diseases, and were weighed weekly.

One of the pleasures of going into the feeding center was that as the weeks and months passed, fewer and fewer children remained there. By the hundreds, we saw starving children graduate from the therapeutic feeding program to the supplemental (70-85 percent of normal body weight) and then be phased out of the feeding program all together. This tangible evidence of success of the program was extremely gratifying to us all.

Sick and hungry as they were, most all of the children responded to any show of affection or interest on our part with smiles that almost melted one's heart. Their smiles made the feeding centers the happiest places at Wad Sherife. If I should remember only one thing about my time in Sudan, I would want to remember the smiles of the children.

Another thing I reflected on during my last week in Kassala was our Fourth of July party. This was totally irrelevant to our purpose of being in Sudan, yet it exemplified how we could enjoy ourselves under any conditions, how we always managed to turn the proverbial sow's ear into a silk purse.

We decorated the house the best we could. On the wall just inside the front door, we hung a large American flag and an old picture postcard of Richard Nixon. Someone had written "Happy 4th of July to you all, Dick" on the postcard. We upgraded the latrine especially for the party, bringing in a small metal table on which we placed a brand new roll of toilet paper, an empty beer bottle with a flower in it, and an old magazine. The only thing missing was a toilet.

We didn't have any beer, either. We settled instead for two cases of Vimto, a British-inspired carbonated fruit-flavored drink; a bottle of *araki*, a bootleg distilled alcohol drink with such a distinctly acquired taste that only Phena could take more than one swallow; and a large bucketful of *marissa*, a thick, faintly alcoholic local brew made from sorghum.

We didn't exactly have a cornucopia of food, either. We had spaghetti without sauce; macaroni with mayonnaise; potato salad made of potatoes, onions and mayo; and a fruit salad of grapefruit, bananas and mangoes.

We had guests from Canada, England, Eritrea, Ireland, Norway, the Philippines, Switzerland and the United States, whose 209th birthday we were celebrating. Bruce Springsteen was there to provide entertainment until an electrical storm blew out the electricity and the tape deck went dead. No electricity also meant no lights but undeterred, we continued by flashlight.

Bob Enik played his guitar the rest of the night and we joined him in singing such American favorites as "House of the Rising Sun" and "White Christmas". Amazingly, just as we began to sing "America the Beautiful," huge bolts of lightning lit up the entire sky. It was a skin-tingling moment. We ended the night around 10:00 or 10:30, well past our usual bedtime, by dancing in the mud under a tree in the garden as lightning continued to flash overhead.

In the very beginning, before my first day at Wad Sherife, I had wondered what I would feel when I saw a refugee camp for the first time. I had been inspired and filled with joy that first day, seeing so many people who had come so far from so many countries to help, all in the spirit of giving, of helping their fellow man at a time when he was unable to help himself.

Now, as I came down to my last day at Wad Sherife, I wondered what I would feel as I departed. When the moment came, I felt terribly uncomfortable. I felt an immense sadness that I was able to leave so freely and that 70,000 others had to stay behind.

ACKNOWLEDGEMENTS

First and foremost, I want to thank my wife Margaret. Had it not been for her support and encouragement, I couldn't have gone to Sudan in the first place, and obviously, there would have been no book.

Thanks to Hugh and Marty Downey, who gave me my first opportunity to work with refugees by signing me on with Lalmba Association. And thanks to Community Hospital of the Monterey Peninsula in Monterey, California, which gave me a leave of absence so I could pursue that opportunity and ensured I'd have a job to return to.

Special thanks to those individuals and organizations whose contributions eased the financial burden of being away from work for six months: my parents, George (now deceased) and Jane Leutzinger; Direct Link; and Monterey doctors J. Mark Bayless, Richard Dauphine, Dennis Evans, David Holley, Walter Holz, William Lewis and Gerald Wyker.

Thanks, too, to my late father-in-law, Bert Wharton, who produced the maps accompanying the text; to Kathy Kubarski, who opened to me her files on international relief agencies at a time when I was first looking for a Third World position; to Peter Bechtold, who advised me on the English phonetic spelling of Sudanese dialect Arabic words; to my friend Glynn Wood of the Monterey Institute for International Studies, who put me in touch with Ms. Kubarski and Prof. Bechtold.

APPENDIX

Some of the background information for this book was obtained from the following sources:

Briefing Packet: Famine in the Non-Government Held Areas of Eritrea and Ethiopia, and Refugees in Eastern Sudan. Interfam Information Project, Khartoum, Sudan, August 1985.

National Geographic, May 1985, pp. 576-633. Journey Up The Nile, by Robert Caputo.

National Geographic, September 1985, pp. 384-404. Eritrea: Region in Rebellion, by Anthony Suau.

Rolling Stone, Dec. 5, 1985, pp. 26-28. Bob Geldof: The Rolling Stone Interview, by D. Breskin.

The International Herald-Tribune, July 29, 1985. Female Circumcision: A Norm in Africa, by Blaine Harden, Washington Post News Service.

The Circumcision Decision, by Edward Wallerstein, The Pennypress, Seattle, Washington.

AFTERNOTE

Ten percent of the author's proceeds from sales of this book will be donated to both Lalmba Association and the American Refugee Committee to help them continue their humanitarian relief efforts in underdeveloped parts of the world.

For current updates on the work they are doing, contact American Refugee Committee, 430 Oak Grove Street, Suite 204, Minneapolis MN 55403, or visit www.archq.org, and Lalmba Association, 7685 Quartz St., Arvada, CO 80007 or www.lalmba.org.

Printed in the United States
44734LVS00002B/548

9 781424 102884